Data Storytelling Secrets

Data Visualization Design for Successful Change-Makers

Oliver Theobald

First Edition

Copyright © 2025 by Oliver Theobald

All rights reserved. No part of this publication may be reproduced, distributed, or transmitted in any form or by any means, including photocopying, recording, or other electronic or mechanical methods, without the prior written permission of the publisher, except in the case of brief quotations embodied in critical reviews and certain other non-commercial uses permitted by copyright law.

ISBN: 9798265701794

TABLE OF CONTENTS

FOREWORD *5*
WHAT IS DATA STORYTELLING? *8*
KNOW YOUR AUDIENCE *13*
FROM QUESTION TO INSIGHT *20*
DATA LITERACY *24*
STORYTELLING *47*
VISUALIZING DATA *61*
DESIGN PRINCIPLES *78*
TOOLS & TECHNIQUES *88*
PRESENTING *97*
FROM ANALYST TO INFLUENCER *105*
TEMPLATES *109*
CHECKLIST *110*
PRACTICE EXERCISES *111*

FOREWORD

We are witnessing a new shift in how we communicate with data. Charts and tables are no longer static summaries buried inside long business reports. Today's tools enable motion, interaction, and narrative pacing in ways that feel closer to media than to spreadsheets. Animated bar chart races, scrolling data essays, and interactive infographics tell a deeper story by demonstrating progression, revealing relationships, and creating emotional impact.

Also, just as filmmakers know how to build suspense, craft resolutions, and evoke emotions, data storytellers know how to guide attention, frame insights, and influence decisions with visual cues. This enables complex ideas to be shared as easily as a story or a viral video. And so, much like how memes reshaped the way people communicate online, data stories are reshaping how people absorb and share information. Most importantly, it gives data the power to do what stories have always done: connect people to meaning.

As the Internet continues to supercharge this new storytelling modality, those who experiment now with the right tools and techniques will be the ones defining the language of data stories in the future. The exciting part is that anyone can craft a compelling data story capable of reaching a wide audience or transforming a business from the inside. The arrival of plug-and-play visualization tools like Flourish and new AI-powered software has made data visualization more accessible than ever before, opening the door to new forms of storytelling. For one, infographics are no longer static; they have evolved into moving, dynamic, and highly shareable formats. Animated bar chart races and scrolling data stories also represent a new medium to consume and share with others.

Online communities show the raw appetite for this type of storytelling. The Reddit forum community r/dataisbeautiful is one of Reddit's most popular, with over 22 million subscribers, ranking 31st in size on Reddit in 2025. Related Reddit communities, including r/infographics, r/mapporn, and r/coolguides, each attract millions more, proving that compelling data visuals resonate with people on a global scale. The "Top 15 Marvel Movies of All Time (2000-2022)" bar chart race video, meanwhile, has attracted over four million views on YouTube.

At the professional level, newsletters and tools are turning data storytelling into high-value ventures. Chartr, a newsletter for visual thinkers, built an audience of over 500,000 readers after launching in 2018 and was later acquired by Robinhood in 2023. Beyond their newsletter, they charge brands upwards of $25,000 for custom storytelling, underlining the demand for strong visuals.

Flourish, founded in 2016, scaled to over 750,000 users by 2022, generating 7.5 million visuals viewed more than 15 billion times. Its acquisition by Canva in 2022 and continued growth to over a million users illustrate the demand for data visualization software.

Individual creators are thriving, too. James Eagle, known for his moving infographics, has built a large following across platforms by repeatedly going viral with his visualizations. App Economy Insights has done the same on Twitter, where its posts often gain tens of thousands of likes. Visual Capitalist has even formalized this trend with a Creator Program, offering direct ways for data storytellers to get paid for their work.

In sum, today's data viz tools don't just help people make charts; they enable them to share ideas at scale, spark conversations, influence industries, and even launch new careers. With the right story, data can travel as widely as any meme, headline, or video clip.

However, while some data storytellers on YouTube and Reddit communities like r/dataisbeautiful are gaining a clear competitive edge, only a small number of people have reached this level. This book aims to fix that by providing you with a practical framework for turning data into stories people actually remember. Whether you're an analyst, marketer, or manager, this book will teach you how to connect the dots between numbers and narrative and be a successful change-maker.

1

WHAT IS DATA STORYTELLING?

We live in a world overflowing with data. Every click, swipe, purchase, and blog post adds to an ever-rising tide of information. Dashboards glow with charts, reports stack up in inboxes, and presentations are packed with bullet points and bar graphs. Yet, amid the torrent of text and numbers, something critical is missing: meaning.

Yes, data is everywhere, but meaning is rare. Just because we have access to data doesn't mean we can process and understand it all. In fact, more often than not, having this much data is overwhelming and counterproductive. It becomes noise and hides the very insights we're trying to uncover. What's needed isn't more information, it's more effective communication. This is where *data storytelling* comes in.

Data storytelling transforms raw numbers into meaning by framing them in a way that people can easily understand and relate to. It does this through the use of three key elements: data, visuals, and narrative.

1. Data is the evidence. It's the foundation that ensures the story is grounded in truth rather than opinion.

2. Visuals translate that evidence into a form the eye and brain can quickly process. This could be charts, maps, and animations.

3. Narrative provides structure. Just as a novelist uses plot, characters, and setting to bring a story to life, a data storyteller uses context and narrative arcs to make information memorable and actionable. A beginning establishes the baseline or context, the middle introduces tension or change, and the end delivers insight, resolution, or action.

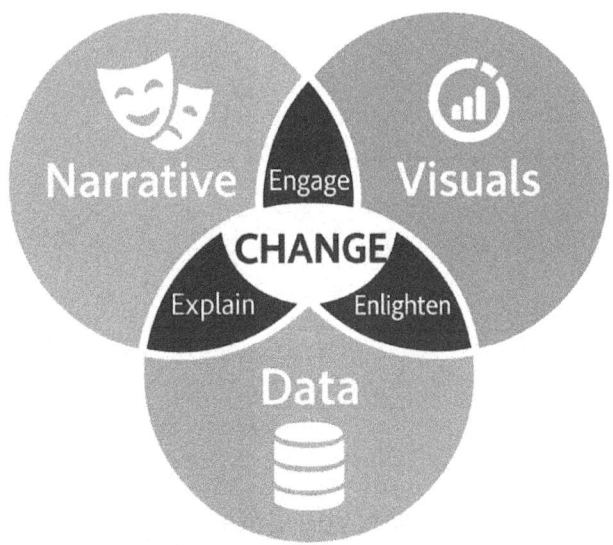

By packaging numbers into narratives, these three elements combine to create an experience that guides the audience through what's happening and provides them with a clear takeaway or course of action. To give you a practical demonstration of this technique, imagine presenting the same information in the following ways.

Version A: Our company's email open rate dropped from 22% to 14% during October and November, but it's now up to 30% as of December.

Version B: For a year, our company's email campaigns held steady with a 22% open rate. However, during a two-month period, that number dropped sharply to 14%. After running A/B tests, we discovered subject line fatigue was the culprit. When we shifted to a new email theme based on trending industry topics, the open rate jumped to 30%. The takeaway?

Refreshing our content regularly is essential to maintaining engagement and a high open rate.

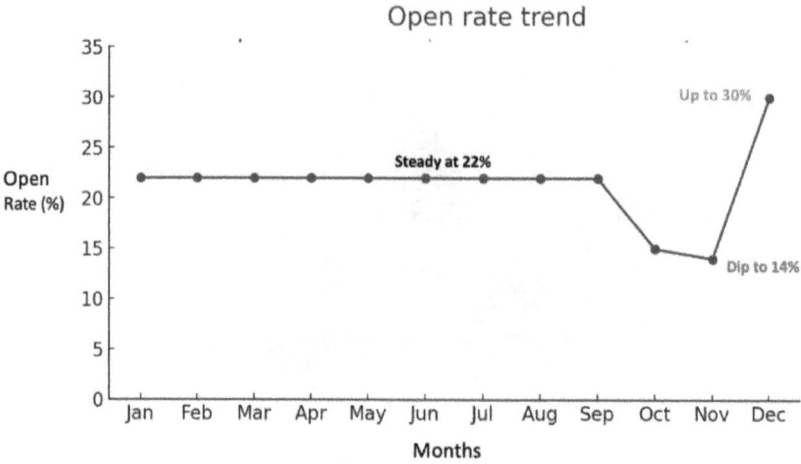

Whereas Version A gives you data, Version B gives you a story and a visualization that you're more likely to remember and act on.

Why storytelling with data matters

In a world driven by metrics and KPIs, storytelling is a highly strategic skill that creates leverage in decision-making. Whether you're an analyst trying to get buy-in from leadership or a product manager making the case for a new feature, the ability to transform raw data into clear, persuasive stories is an important skill to get ahead and drive change.

What makes data storytelling so powerful is efficiency. A well-designed graph or moving infographic can be worth a thousand words. By saving audiences time while delivering depth, these new tools create messages that spread faster and stick longer.

We also live in the era of data-driven decision-making, where the loudest opinion no longer wins. Decisions must be grounded in evidence and communicated through narratives that make them clear and persuasive. This is because numbers by themselves rarely change minds—but stories do. Why? Because the human brain is wired for stories, not spreadsheets. We remember narratives, not charts, and we respond to emotion, not just logic. Research in neuroscience suggests that stories activate more areas of the brain than raw facts alone. When we hear facts, only the language-processing centers light up, but when we hear a story—especially one involving people, emotions, or movement—our sensory and emotional centers are engaged too. This creates a richer, more immersive experience. That's why we remember stories more vividly and act on them more often.

Put simply, a well-told story can make an insight stick and move someone to act. However, storytelling with data doesn't mean manipulation or hiding contradicting evidence. It's about providing clarity and bringing structure, emotion, context, and relevance to complex information. It helps decision-makers see what matters and why it matters now.

Lastly and most importantly, it's about trust. When data is presented poorly, lacks context, or is manipulated to fit a desired narrative, people stop believing it. Audiences are quick to sense when numbers are being cherry-picked or when a chart is designed to mislead. Credibility, once lost, is hard to recover. A compelling data story, on the other hand, builds trust because it shows you understand not only the numbers but also the context, limitations, and implications behind them. It reassures the audience that you've done the work, weighed the evidence, and are presenting insights honestly. Trust, therefore, doesn't come from dazzling visuals or complex analysis alone; it comes from clarity, transparency, and respect for the bigger picture that gives those numbers meaning.

In the next chapter, we'll dive into the single most overlooked skill in data communication: understanding your audience. A story that inspires one group can fall flat with another—which is why tailoring your message is just as important as the data itself.

Key takeaways

• We live in a world overflowing with data, but meaning is often missing.

• Data storytelling combines data, visuals, and narrative to make insights

more engaging, memorable, and actionable.

• Data storytelling is not about manipulation or hiding the truth.

2

KNOW YOUR AUDIENCE

If you want your data story to resonate, you have to start with your audience, not the data. This might sound counterintuitive, especially if you've spent hours cleaning datasets or fine-tuning models. But even the most brilliant analysis falls flat if it isn't tailored to the right audience.

Before generating any charts, you first need to ask: Who am I talking to? What do they care about? What blind spots might they have? What is the one idea they will remember as they walk out of the room? What language do they speak—technical, strategic, and/or visual?

The level of data literacy of your audience plays a big role. Not everyone can easily interpret standard deviation and three-dimensional scatterplots. What is obvious to you may not be to someone else. The responsibility is on you, not your audience, to bridge the gap between technical details and understanding.

In most situations, simplification is your greatest tool. The CEO doesn't want a regression analysis; they want to know if the company is on track. A marketing director doesn't want p-values; they want to know which campaign drove results. Your job as the storyteller is to meet them where they are, not drag them into your world.

Categories of decision-makers

To be an effective data storyteller, you should be able to identify and understand three core audience types:

executive, managerial, and technical. Each audience category processes information differently, values different details, and requires a tailored approach to ensure the data story actually resonates and drives action.

Executives, for example, seek clarity and relevance. They have limited time and focus on outcomes, so you need to lead with the "so what"—the insight, the decision, or the recommendation. Keep the story high-level, visually clean, and actionable.

Managers sit in the middle. They care about both the outcome and the reasoning behind it. They appreciate context and some of the data trail, but not excessive detail. For this audience, add supporting evidence while keeping the narrative moving.

Technical audiences are comfortable with detail and methodology. This is your chance to show the work—assumptions, confidence intervals, and model logic. Still, don't lose the narrative thread, even technical experts need help connecting the dots.

Executive	Managers	Technical
Customer retention dropped 12%, putting $5M in revenue at risk.	Customer retention dropped 12%, putting $5M in revenue at risk. **The decline is concentrated among mobile users after our last app update.**	Customer retention dropped 12%, putting $5M in revenue at risk. The decline is concentrated among mobile users after our last app update. **Here's the regression analysis showing feature adoption as the strongest predictor of churn.**

As a practical demonstration, imagine you're presenting churn data. If you are presenting to executives, you would highlight that: "Customer retention dropped 12%, putting $5M in revenue at risk." For managers, you'd add context: "The decline is concentrated among mobile users after our last app update." For technical teams, you'd go deeper: "Here's the regression analysis showing feature adoption as the strongest predictor of churn." The same dataset, but three different stories—each tailored to a specific audience.

Beyond these three audience categories, it's critical to understand your people's emotional stakes, too. What do they fear? What do they hope for? Even accurate data can be rejected if it challenges someone's worldview or threatens their priorities. People don't resist numbers; they resist feeling misunderstood. Empathy, therefore, is your most underrated storytelling skill.

As an example, imagine you're presenting cost-cutting data to an executive team. A CFO might welcome the results, since higher profit margins reduce financial risk. But the Head of HR could react very differently, worrying that cost-cutting means staff layoffs. The same data looks positive to one leader and threatening to another because each person sees it through their own priorities. Thus, even if your analysis is accurate, the reaction to it will differ depending on the emotional stakes of the audience. By acknowledging those concerns—perhaps by pairing efficiency gains with a plan to reskill rather than reduce staff—you'll be able to build more trust and buy-in.

Tone of voice

Another important consideration is the tone of your data story. Tone is a subtle but powerful tool for shaping perception. The same chart can land differently depending on the tone you use to frame it. A celebratory voice can make progress feel like a shared victory: "This quarter we hit a milestone we've been chasing for two years." A serious voice, on the other hand, can underscore urgency and risk: "The decline in customer satisfaction, if left unaddressed, threatens our long-term retention."

The tone signals to the audience how they should interpret what they're seeing—whether to feel encouraged, concerned, optimistic, or cautious. The best storytellers align tone with message so that the emotional tone supports the data's message. Conversely, a mismatch between the data and the tone is likely to cause confusion. Imagine announcing a budget shortfall with cheerful energy, or describing record-breaking sales in a flat, monotone way. A technical memo might be best written in a neutral, objective voice. A presentation to a product team might benefit from energy and curiosity. A warning about risk might need urgency and seriousness. All of these tone choices flow from who your audience is and what the moment requires.

Another factor is familiarity. When you're presenting to a familiar audience, such as colleagues you meet with regularly, you can adopt a more conversational style and move quickly through the background information. For a new audience, though, you don't yet have the advantage of established trust. How you present your data—your choice of tone and level of confidence—often signals whether you can be relied upon. If the tone suggests care, professionalism, and respect for the audience's perspective, the story is more likely to resonate with a new audience.

Lastly, good data storytelling doesn't always require one consistent tone throughout. Just as a novel shifts between tension and release, your presentation might open with gravity, pivot to optimism once a solution is identified, and close with confidence about the path ahead. By adjusting your voice with intention, you keep the audience emotionally attuned to the story's narrative arc.

Tone	Example wording
Celebratory	We achieved a milestone this quarter, surpassing our revenue target for the first time in two years.
Serious	The decline in customer satisfaction poses a risk to long-term retention and requires immediate attention.
Urgent	If we don't address this drop in conversion rates now, we risk losing market share within the next quarter.
Optimistic	The recent uptick in engagement signals that our new strategy is starting to take hold.
Cautious	While the numbers look promising, we need more data before confirming this as a sustained trend.
Confident	The evidence is clear: this approach works, and we should scale it across the business.
Neutral/Analytical	Engagement increased 12% compared to last quarter, with the largest gains coming from mobile users.

Timing

Next, let's talk about timing. Every story has a right moment. You can have the perfect insight, the right data, and even a compelling narrative—but if you share it at the wrong time, it won't land. A quarterly business review, for instance, might not be the right time for deep experimentation results. A brainstorming session probably isn't the moment to dwell on last quarter's performance metrics. Knowing when to tell a story is just as important as how.

Timing operates on several layers. Every organization has its own cadence—weekly team huddles, monthly planning, quarterly board reviews—and the data story needs to match the rhythm of reporting. A board meeting, for instance, calls for strategic patterns and long-term implications, not daily fluctuations.

The decision window is just as important. Data carries the most weight when it intersects with choices that are about to be made. If a pricing review is scheduled for next week, that is the moment when customer sensitivity data has the power to shift strategy. Miss that window, and even the sharpest insight may feel irrelevant.

There is an emotional dimension to timing, too. Audiences are not blank slates; they bring moods and expectations into the room. Pitching a bold new growth experiment immediately after a disappointing quarter can make it sound reckless, while the same idea presented after a small win might feel energizing and achievable. Even within a single presentation, timing shapes impact. Opening with background noise, such as disclaimers, overly detailed methodology explanations, and too much background context, risks losing attention before you arrive at the key message. Instead, leading with the key message and then layering in context ensures that the audience hears what matters most while they are still fully engaged.

Ultimately, storytelling with data starts with listening to the people the data is for. When you know your audience, you can choose the right narrative, the right visual, the right tone, and the right timing.

In the next chapter, we'll move from people to problems and explore how to turn questions into insights that help drive your story in the right direction.

Key takeaways

• Start with your audience, not the data. Speak their language and priorities.
• Different decision-makers need different stories. Executives want clarity and action, managers want context and reasoning, and technical audiences want detail and methodology.
• Match your voice (i.e., celebratory, urgent, neutral) to the message and the audience to ensure it lands as intended.

- Timing matters. Even a great story can fail at the wrong moment.

3

FROM QUESTION TO INSIGHT

Every good data story starts with a leading question. This is a question that gives your story purpose. Think of this question as the backbone of your narrative. It defines the edges of your exploration and tells you what to include and what to ignore.

Without that question, curiosity can lead you to collect everything—every metric, every graph, every dataset. But curiosity alone can drown you in noise. Clarity comes when you use questions as a filter. Each slide, each visualization, and each sentence should be a response to a question the audience cares about. Without that spine, your story risks collapsing into a collection of disconnected numbers and a wandering exercise in chart-making.

However, not all questions are created equal. Some questions point you toward relevant insight, while others only generate noise, as we'll explore in this chapter.

Asking good questions

Good questioning is a discipline in itself, and it begins with understanding the business context. What decision is on the line? What tension or uncertainty needs to be resolved? What levers for action might exist?

Sometimes, the best questions often arise from tension. Somewhere between what you know and what you need to know lies the gap where insight hides. If you frame your analysis without recognizing that tension—between strategy and execution, between expectations and outcomes—you risk collecting data that only reinforces what you already believe, instead of uncovering something new.

Imagine a marketing team whose campaign strategy predicted a 10% increase in sign-ups but only delivered 3%. The gap between expectation and outcome creates tension. The valuable question to ask isn't "How do we explain away the shortfall?" but "What caused it? Was it the targeting? The message? The channel? Or something in the customer journey?" The former looks for a justification. Its purpose is to make the results seem less damaging, to smooth things over, or to find excuses. For example, someone might say, "Sign-ups were low because the economy was tough." While that explanation may be true, it doesn't open the door to deeper learning or actionable insight.

The latter and alternative line of questioning pushes analysis toward discovery rather than justification. It forces you to go beyond surface-level numbers and dig into the drivers behind them. Otherwise, you might only collect data that confirms your original assumptions instead of discovering what truly went wrong.

Next, a good question should narrow your field of vision without blinding you. It should be clear enough to guide your next step, but open enough to let surprising patterns emerge. Poor questions, on the other hand, either cast the net too wide ("What does the data say?") or are framed so narrowly that the answer is predetermined ("Can we prove campaign A outperformed campaign B?").

Open-ended	Focused
How is our marketing performing?	Which channels contributed the most to Q2 revenue growth?
What do customers think?	What feedback patterns appear in the past 90 days of support tickets?
Are our employees engaged?	How did employee engagement scores change in the last two surveys?
How is our website doing?	Which landing page had the highest conversion rate last quarter?

By framing your analysis around sharper questions, you not only uncover better insights—you can also tell a story that resonates. The key is to move from open-ended curiosity to focused inquiry. Instead of asking, "How is our marketing performing?", ask "Which channels contributed the most to Q2 revenue growth?" Instead of "What do customers think?", ask "What feedback pattern appears most in the past 90 days of support tickets?"

Finally, remember that a question is not just for you—it's for your audience. A great data story anticipates the questions in their minds and aligns your framing with their concerns. Executives care less about the intricacies of a regression model and more about whether to double the ad budget. A product manager wants to know not just what feature is underperforming, but what trade-offs exist in fixing it. Tailoring your questions to the audience ensures that your insights don't just inform—they influence.

One way to sharpen your questions is to test them against these three filters:

1. Is it specific?

A vague question like "How are things going with our marketing?" doesn't give enough direction to analyze. Reframe it as "Which channels contributed most to Q2 revenue growth?" and you immediately narrow the scope to something focused and answerable.

2. Does it focus on what you can measure?

Lofty questions like "How do we make customers happier?" may inspire brainstorming, but they don't give you a measurable target. Reframe them as "Which customer service issues account for the largest share of complaints this quarter?" and suddenly the path to analysis and evidence is easier to find.

3. Does it open the door to action?

If the story isn't relevant to the target audience and won't influence what the business does next, it's not worth asking. Data storytelling isn't about entertainment, it's about decisions—unless you are specifically generating data stories for online media consumption.

Together, these filters help separate vague prompts from questions that actually drive insight. For instance, "Why did customer churn increase in Q2?" is specific to a key business problem, can be explored and diagnosed with evidence, and directs attention toward decisions that could reduce churn. "What are the biggest drivers of customer loyalty in our mobile app?" also gives direction without assuming the answer. In contrast, "Let's see what's in the numbers" leads nowhere, because there's no defined problem to solve.

Key takeaways

• Every strong data story begins with a clear question that defines focus and direction.

• Sometimes the best questions come from the tension between what you know and what you need to know.

• Audience matters, so frame questions around what your stakeholders need to know, not just what interests you.

• Filters help sharpen questions. Make it specific, focus on what you can measure, and open the door to action.

4

DATA LITERACY

Numbers are persuasive—but only when they're properly understood. A good chart can end an argument, a percentage change can shift strategy, and a new dataset can influence an entire industry. Yet every figure hides the risk of misinterpretation. A small sample might exaggerate, a selective time frame might distort, and a simple correlation might be mistaken for causation.

This makes data literacy crucial to overall success. Without literacy, data is decoration: polished on the surface but fragile under scrutiny. Data literacy, though, isn't about mastering advanced statistics or building complex models. It's about asking the right questions of the data in front of you. Are the variables defined properly? Is the trend line steady or exponential? Is this finding exploratory or explanatory? Is the signal real, or just noise dressed up as insight?

In this chapter, we'll break down the essentials—covering variables and relationships, linear and exponential growth, correlation and causation, and the importance of time frames and sample size.

Variables: The building blocks of data

At a basic level, data is a collection of variables—measurable characteristics about something that can change or vary from one case to another. These variables are the building blocks for data analysis because they capture different aspects of what you're attempting to measure, analyze, and understand.

To see how this plays out in practice, think of a dataset as a table: each column represents a variable, and each row shows its value for a specific item. For example, in a customer survey, age might be one variable, satisfaction rating another, and number of purchases a third. What makes them "variables" is that they don't stay the same— different customers can be older or younger, more or less satisfied, and buy more or fewer products. One customer might be 22 years old, rate their satisfaction as 8 out of 10, and have made 3 purchases, while another might be 47 years old, rate their satisfaction as 5 out of 10, and have made 12 purchases. The richness of data comes from these differences across cases as they reveal patterns, outliers, and other relationships. By comparing how variables change together—such as whether higher satisfaction tends to correspond with more purchases, or whether age affects buying behavior—we can begin to generate insights.

Customer	Age (years)	Satisfaction (1–10)	Purchases
A	22	8	3
B	47	5	12
C	35	9	7
D	29	6	2
E	53	4	10

However, not all variables play the same role in analysis. Understanding how variables function is critical because their roles determine the types of questions you can ask and the methods you use to answer them. For instance, variables are often classified into dependent and independent categories.

Independent variables are the factors you can control or observe as given conditions. They do not depend on other variables in the analysis. Dependent variables, on the other hand, are the outcomes that respond to changes in those independent factors. For example, in a marketing campaign, ad spend is the independent variable because you decide how much to invest. Conversions are the dependent variable because they shift up or down depending on the ad spend. In retail, factors like store location, product price, or day of the week can be independent variables, while daily revenue is the dependent variable that reflects how those factors play out.

This distinction is important because it moves analysis beyond simply describing numbers and toward explaining the relationships. If you only focus on dependent variables, then you are only describing what happened. This could be reporting that sales increased by 15% this quarter, that customer satisfaction averaged 4.2 out of 5, or that website traffic peaked on Tuesdays. To explain why something happened, however, you need to consider independent variables—the inputs or causes that drive those outcomes—and explore their relationships to a dependent variable. For example, sales might have risen because the sales team was expanded, higher satisfaction scores may be linked to faster response times, or Tuesday traffic peaks may coincide with weekly email campaigns. In these cases, the independent variable defines the intervention, while the dependent variable measures the outcome.

In practice, data storytelling usually focuses on one dependent variable at a time — the single outcome you want to explain or predict. While advanced methods can handle multiple outcomes, keeping the focus on one makes the relationship clearer and easier to understand.

In sum, descriptive analysis focuses only on dependent variables, such as reporting that sales grew 15% this quarter or that customer satisfaction averaged 4.2 out of 5. These observations explain the "what" but stop short of addressing the "why." Explanatory analysis, by contrast, examines how independent variables—the inputs or drivers—affect the dependent variable, which is the outcome.

Lastly, it's important to realize that variables don't always play a fixed role. A variable that acts as an outcome in one context can serve as a driver in another.

Consider customer satisfaction. In one study, it may be treated as a dependent variable influenced by response time, employee friendliness, or product quality. In another analysis, satisfaction itself becomes an independent variable, shaping outcomes such as repeat purchases, customer loyalty, or brand advocacy.

The same concept applies in health studies: exercise might be analyzed as a dependent variable (influenced by income, education, or environment), but it can also be an independent factor affecting weight, mood, or long-term health outcomes.

Recognizing that variables can change roles helps analysts avoid oversimplification. It also emphasizes the importance of clearly defining the research question. What is the variable of interest? What are the hypothesized drivers? What outcomes are being measured? Framing the analysis properly ensures that the relationships drawn are valid and that the conclusions support actionable insights.

Data types: How variables are measured

Variables not only differ in their role as independent or dependent, but also in how they are measured and recorded. This matters because the type of variable dictates what kinds of questions you can ask, which statistical methods are valid, and which visualizations will make sense.

At a high level, variables can be split into quantitative variables and qualitative variables.

Quantitative variables represent numerical measurements, which can be further divided into two forms:

1. Continuous variables that can take any numeric value (i.e., temperature, weight, time spent on website).

2. Discrete variables that can only take whole number values (i.e., items purchased, page views). You can't have, for example, 5.5 company cars or 3.3 clicks.

Qualitative variables, meanwhile, represent categories or groups and can be nominal or ordinal.

1. Nominal categories have no natural order (i.e., colors, product categories, geographic regions).

2. Ordinal categories have a meaningful order (i.e., satisfaction ratings from "poor" to "excellent," education levels, company sizes from "small" to "large").

In the following table, you can see examples of all four types of variables.

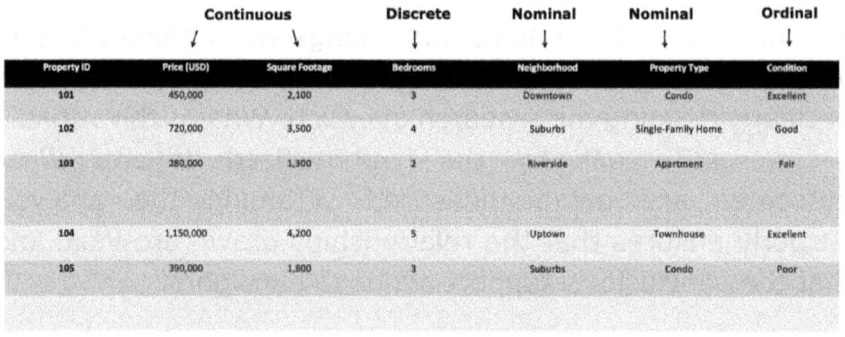

Note that the first column, Property ID, is not technically a variable. Even though it's numeric, you wouldn't analyze it like price or square footage. Its only purpose is to identify each unique property in the dataset.

Understanding different variable types directly impacts how you analyze and present your data. For data analysis, you can calculate averages like the mean (average value) or median (the middle value) for continuous variables, but not for nominal ones. You can rank ordinal variables, but not nominal ones. You can perform regression analysis with continuous variables, but not with categorical data. For data visualization, continuous variables work well for line charts and scatterplots. Categorical variables, meanwhile, are better suited for bar charts and pie charts.

The following table breaks down which type of analysis is possible using different types of variables.

Analysis Method	Continuous	Discrete	Nominal	Ordinal
Median	Yes	Yes	Limited (only binary)	Yes
Mean	Yes	Yes (if numeric)	No	Not ideal
Pearson Correlation	Yes	Yes (if numeric)	No	No
Spearman Correlation	Yes	Yes	No	Yes
Standard Deviation	Yes	Yes (if numeric)	No	Rarely used (not recommended)

Let's now look in detail at each analysis method highlighted in the table, starting with the median.

1. Median

The median is the middle value when data is arranged in order from smallest to largest. For example, if property prices are $250,000, $400,000, and $450,000, the median is $400,000 because that is the middle data point (with a lower and higher data point on either side). If there were four data points, the median would be the value of the second and third data points divided by two (i.e., ($400,000 + $410,000)/2 = $405,000).

For a visual demonstration of the median, the following scatterplot shows five property prices as data points, with the red dashed line marking the median value of $400,000.

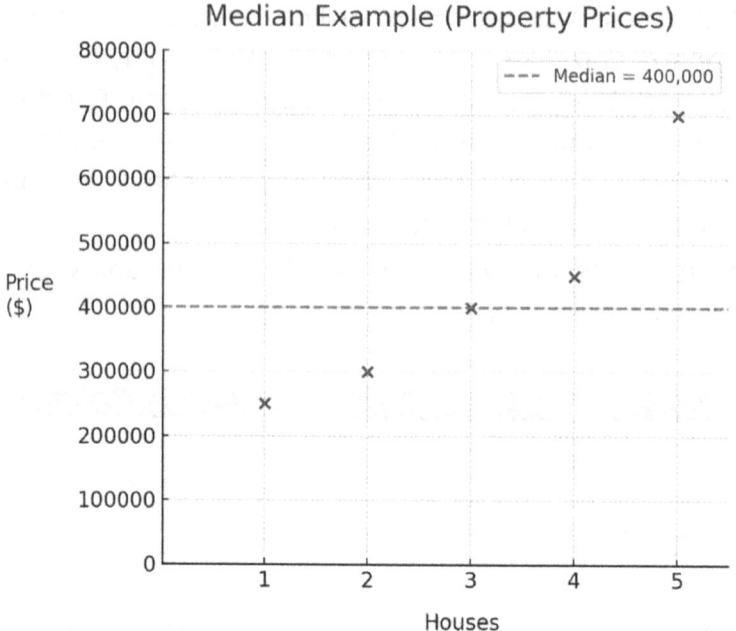

Medians work with continuous and discrete variables because the values can be easily ordered and the central point can therefore be identified. Ordinal variables also support medians because their categories possess a natural order, such as "poor," "fair," "good," and "excellent." Conversely, the median cannot be found for more than two nominal variables because categories like "red," "blue," or "green" have no inherent order and there is no middle value.

For binary nominal variables, the median can technically be defined if the two categories are coded as 0 and 1. The median value will be whichever category occurs more often, as the middle of the distribution falls where most values lie. Still, statisticians usually don't recommend using the median for binary nominal data, even though it can still be computed. They typically prefer using the mode method, which is another measure of the middle that simply identifies the most common value in the dataset.

2. Mean

The mean, or average, is different from the median because it's calculated as the sum of all values divided by the number of observations. For instance, with square footage values of 1,000, 1,500, and 2,500, the mean value is 1,666.6. Means are appropriate for continuous and discrete variables because these are numbers you can easily measure and calculate.

In the chart below, there are five property prices as bars, with the red dashed line at $420,000 representing the mean.

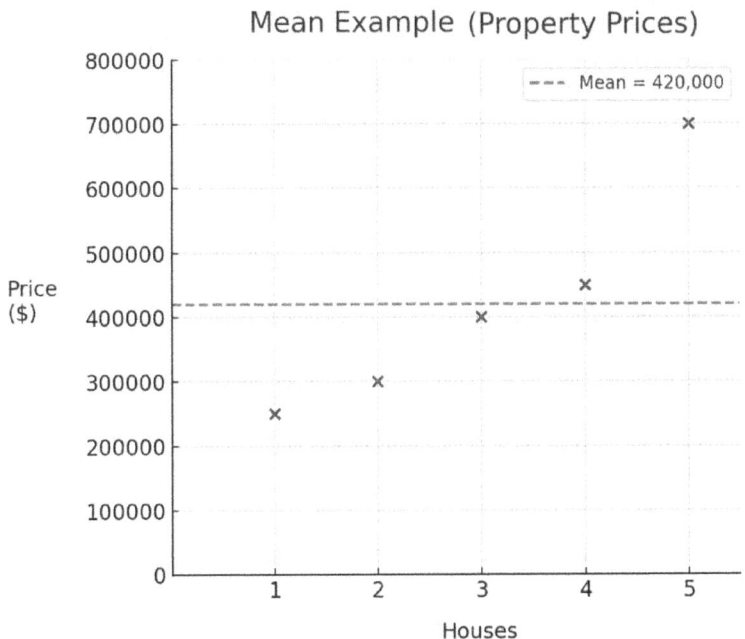

With ordinal variables, means can be computed if numeric codes are assigned, but the result is misleading since the spacing between categories is not consistent. For example, the difference between "poor" and "fair" is not necessarily the same as the difference between "fair" and "good." For nominal data, a mean cannot be calculated at all because the categories do not represent quantities.

3. Pearson Correlation

Pearson correlation measures the strength and direction of a linear relationship between two numeric variables. The result is expressed as a value between −1 and +1, known as the correlation coefficient (written as r). This tells you whether two variables rise and fall together in a straight-line pattern, move in opposite directions, or show no consistent relationship at all. For example, property price and square footage generally show a positive correlation greater than 0 because larger homes usually cost more. Conversely, price and distance from the city center might show a negative correlation, since properties farther away typically cost less. A value near 0 suggests little to no linear relationship.

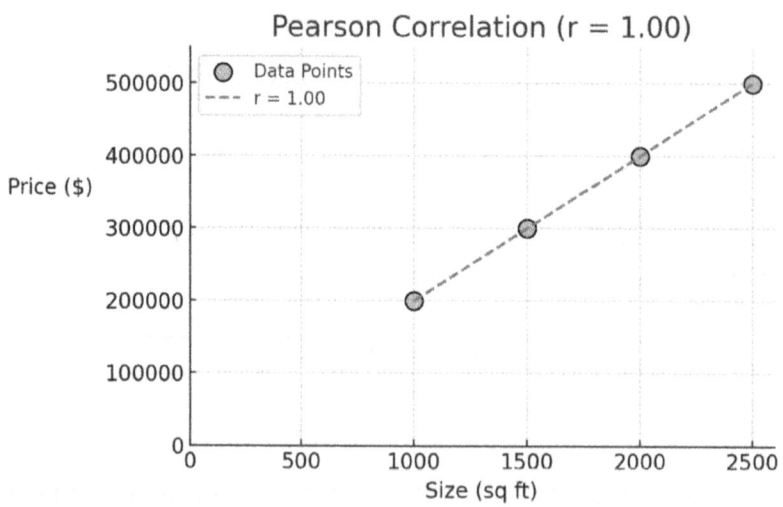

The scatterplot above plots home size against price, with the points lying perfectly on a straight upward line equivalent to r = 1.00. The data points illustrate a perfect positive Pearson correlation, with r = 1.00, between home size and price. This means that as the size of a home increases, the price increases in exact proportion, forming a perfectly straight upward line. In reality, housing data almost never aligns this perfectly, but this example demonstrates what a flawless linear relationship looks like.

Lastly, Pearson correlation is appropriate only for continuous and discrete variables where values are numerical and equally spaced. It does not apply to nominal variables because categories cannot be translated into numbers in a meaningful way. Ordinal variables are also unsuitable because the differences between categories are not equal. In these cases, Spearman correlation is used instead.

4. Spearman Correlation

Spearman correlation measures the strength and direction of the relationship between two variables based on their ranks, rather than their exact values. Just like Pearson, Spearman correlation is expressed as a value between -1 and +1, but it is denoted by the Greek letter ρ (rho) instead of r.

The key difference is that Pearson looks for a straight-line (linear) relationship, while Spearman only requires that the relationship be monotonic. A monotonic pattern means the variables move consistently in one direction—either always upward or always downward—but not necessarily at a constant pace or in a perfectly straight line. In other words, as one variable goes up, the other usually goes up (or usually goes down), but the pace of change doesn't have to be steady (linear).

For example, property price and distance from the city center may not follow a perfect straight-line decline—prices might drop quickly at first and then level off—but they still generally move in opposite directions. Spearman correlation captures this consistent upward or downward trend, even when the pattern is curved or uneven.

Spearman correlation is therefore useful for ordinal data, where categories have an order but not equal spacing, and for continuous data that do not meet the assumptions required for Pearson correlation because the data is non-linear, skewed, or contains extreme outliers.

As an example, the following plot shows the distance from the city center against price, showing a perfect downward trend where greater distance corresponds to lower prices (ρ = −1.00).

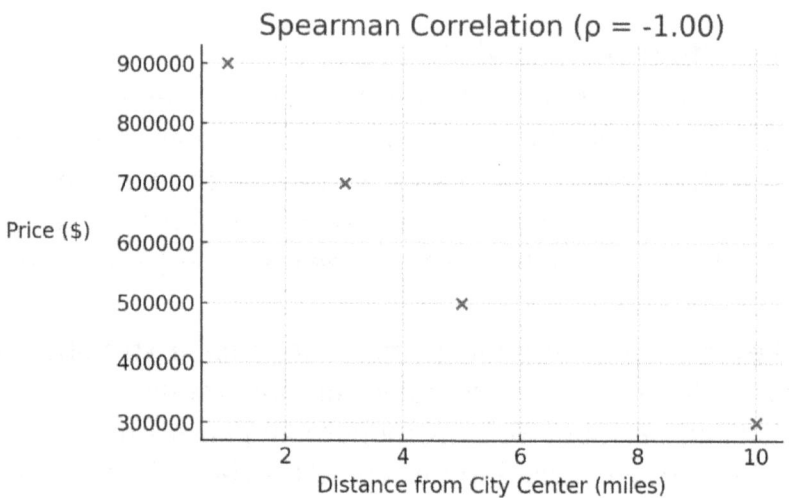

Here, as the distance from the city center increases, property prices fall consistently. While not entirely linear, the points form a perfectly monotonic downward pattern: the farthest homes from the city are always the least expensive, and the closest homes are always the most expensive.

5. Standard Deviation

When we describe a dataset, knowing the average is only part of the story. Two groups of numbers can have the same mean but look completely different depending on how tightly or loosely the values are spread. This is where standard deviation comes in. It measures the amount of variation around the average and shows whether your data points cluster closely together or are widely scattered.

For example, two neighborhoods may both have an average property price of $500,000, but if one ranges from $300,000 to $700,000 and the other from $480,000 to $520,000, the first neighborhood has greater variation and therefore a higher standard deviation. Even though both neighborhoods share the same average value of $500,000, the first neighborhood has more variation in price, which results in a higher standard deviation. This is why standard deviation adds an extra layer of insight beyond the average—it reveals the stability or volatility in the data.

Standard deviation works well for continuous and discrete numeric data, but not for ordinal data where gaps between categories are uneven, and not at all for nominal data, which carry no numerical meaning.

Summary

When you encounter any dataset, start by identifying:

1. What are the variables being measured?
2. Are you trying to describe what happened or explain why it happened?
3. Which variables are independent (potential causes) and which are dependent (potential effects)?

4. What type of data is each variable (continuous, discrete, nominal, ordinal)?

These questions will guide your entire analysis approach and help you choose appropriate methods for exploring and analyzing your data.

Common variable pitfalls

Working with variables is central to data analysis, but it also comes with traps that can distort conclusions if not properly managed. Misinterpreting relationships, overlooking hidden influences, or failing to recognize how variables shift roles can all lead to misleading stories.

One of the most dangerous mistakes in data storytelling is confusing correlation with causation. The terms sound similar, but they represent very different relationships.

Causation means that one variable directly influences another, and changing the first variable produces a measurable effect on the second. Correlation, by contrast, means that two variables move together in some way. However, this doesn't mean that one is causing the other to change. Correlation is about patterns, not proof.

As an example, ice cream sales and drowning incidents both rise in the summer. But that doesn't mean ice cream causes drowning. Instead, a third factor—hot weather—drives both patterns. Similarly, studies often show a correlation between heavy social media use and higher levels of anxiety. But does scrolling cause anxiety, or are anxious people more likely to spend time online? Without careful research design, it's impossible to know for sure.

For data storytellers, the danger comes from overstating what the numbers show. A chart with two rising lines can look convincing, but correlation alone is not proof of cause. Sometimes what appears to be a direct link between two variables is actually driven by a third, hidden factor.

Hidden variables—also called confounding variables—are factors that influence both variables in their correlation but remain unseen in the initial analysis. They can create the illusion of a direct relationship when, in reality, a third element is driving both. If you notice that stores with red signs have higher sales, the color might not be the cause—perhaps red-signed stores are larger or in better locations.

The risk of hidden variables is especially common in observational data, where researchers cannot control all conditions. Without accounting for these influences, decision-makers might act on misleading conclusions. For instance, if a retailer repainted all its stores red based on the correlation, it might spend heavily with little impact on sales.

This makes it important to ask whether a hidden variable or a simple coincidence might explain the pattern. Strong data storytellers know that credibility comes not from bold claims, but from careful, honest framing.

Data dimensionality

Modern datasets are rarely simple. Instead of dealing with one or two variables, analysts today often face dozens or even hundreds—spanning demographics, customer behaviors, product features, and marketing channels. This complexity is called *dimensionality*. The more variables, the higher the dimensionality, and the harder it becomes to separate what really matters from what is just noise.

Take customer churn as an example. If more customers are leaving, is the cause higher prices, poor service quality, aggressive competitor activity, seasonal shifts, or some combination of these factors? When many variables interact at once, it's easy to find patterns that appear meaningful but are actually misleading.

Spotify, for example, deals with enormous dimensionality when recommending songs. Its algorithms analyze dozens of factors at once—tempo, genre, artist, listening time, user skips, and even the time of day you're listening. Without careful filtering, the system could recommend irrelevant songs because of spurious correlations. By prioritizing the variables most predictive of user enjoyment, Spotify transforms all this complexity into clear, tailored recommendations.

In practice, this same principle applies to data storytelling. Whether it's grouping related factors, focusing on the top two or three drivers, or visualizing the strongest relationships, the key is to respect the richness of the dataset while focusing on the most relevant variables.

Sample size and representativeness

Before drawing conclusions from data, it's worth asking a simple but powerful question: How many observations does this conclusion rest on, and do they reflect the bigger picture? A statistic is only as reliable as the data behind it. If your sample size is too small, random noise can masquerade as a meaningful trend. For example, a survey of just 20 customers might suggest a dramatic swing in satisfaction levels, but the results are meaningless without scale. Small numbers amplify chance variation, producing stories that collapse once broader data is collected.

Equally important is representativeness. A large sample can be misleading if it doesn't reflect the population you want to understand. A survey of only your most loyal customers will paint a rosy picture, but it won't explain why new customers are leaving. Similarly, a dataset skewed toward one demographic, region, or behavior can hide the experiences of others, producing biased conclusions.

For example, imagine a weight-loss app releasing survey data claiming that "most users reported dramatic improvements in health within weeks." Later scrutiny might reveal that the survey only included a few hundred of the app's most engaged, motivated users—while thousands of casual sign-ups who quickly dropped off were excluded. The story told would be technically accurate for that small, loyal subset, but not representative of the broader customer base. Once those limitations became clear, trust in the brand's messaging would erode.

These examples underscore the danger of overlooking sample size and representativeness. For data storytellers, the key questions are: Is this sample large enough? And is it representative of the audience I'm trying to describe? Without both, a story risks sounding confident but being fundamentally flawed.

Time frames & cherry-picking data

The time frame you choose can dramatically shape the story the data appears to tell. A one-month sales dip may look alarming in isolation, but when viewed against a five-year upward trend, it is little more than a seasonal fluctuation. Conversely, highlighting only a strong quarter while ignoring years of stagnation paints an unrealistically positive picture.

This is where cherry picking becomes dangerous. Cherry picking happens when data is selectively presented to support a desired conclusion while ignoring the broader context. It can be intentional—meant to persuade—or unintentional, the result of failing to zoom out and examine the full picture. Either way, it is one of the quickest ways to undermine credibility.

A data-literate storyteller recognizes that time frames matter. They deliberately choose ranges that provide context, acknowledge exceptions, and present a balanced view of both short-term fluctuations and long-term patterns.

Imagine a major streaming service reporting a strong quarter of subscriber growth and framing it as proof of renewed momentum. Headlines might celebrate the "turnaround," and the stock price could briefly climb. Yet a closer look could reveal that the company had lost millions of subscribers earlier in the year and that the overall 12-month trend still pointed downward. By spotlighting a narrow time frame, the company would create a short-lived success narrative—one that could quickly unravel once the full context came to light. Such a scenario serves as a cautionary example of how selective framing can undermine investor trust.

Credible storytelling demands that we present the full arc of the data, not just the chapter that fits the story we want to tell.

Linear vs. exponential change

Not all change is equal, and recognizing the difference between types of change is one of the most crucial skills in data literacy. That's because the way something grows or declines over time tells an important story. Misreading that story can lead to catastrophic business decisions or missed opportunities.

First, let's examine the basic tenets of linear and exponential growth.

Linear change: The steady march

Linear change refers to growth or decline that progresses at a constant rate. In other words, the same amount is added or subtracted during each time period. Due to its consistency, linear change is relatively easy to model.

In charts, linear patterns appear as straight lines. The slope tells you the rate of change. Steeper slopes indicate faster linear growth, while gentler slopes show slower linear growth. A flat line, meanwhile, signals no change at all.

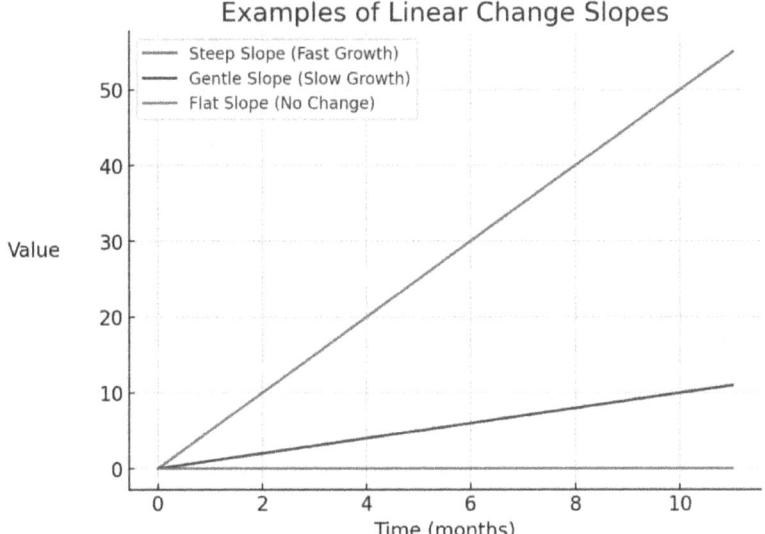

(Note that this chart has extra margin around the minimum values. This is called axis margin, and it prevents lines or markers from sitting flush against the border, which would make them harder to see, as is the case for the Flat Slope line in this example.)

Linear change is easy to predict, plan for, and understand. It works well in environments where growth or decline happens in controlled, measured increments, such as budgeting, staffing plans, recurring expenses, or gradual improvements. If your monthly revenue increases by $10,000 each month, you can confidently project that in six months, there will be a gain of $60,000 in additional monthly revenue.

Here are four other examples of linear change:

- Sales increase by $10,000 each month.
- A company hires 5 new employees every quarter.
- Manufacturing costs rise by $2 per unit each year due to inflation.

- Website traffic grows by 100 visitors per week.

Exponential change: The compounding force

Exponential change describes growth or decline that accelerates over time. Instead of adding the same fixed amount in each period, exponential change multiplies by the same factor. This multiplication creates a compounding effect, where each new step builds on all previous changes.

For example, if users double every month, growth moves from 10 to 20 to 40 to 80 to 160. In the first few months, the increase may seem small, but the numbers soon explode. This "hockey stick" shape is the hallmark of exponential growth.

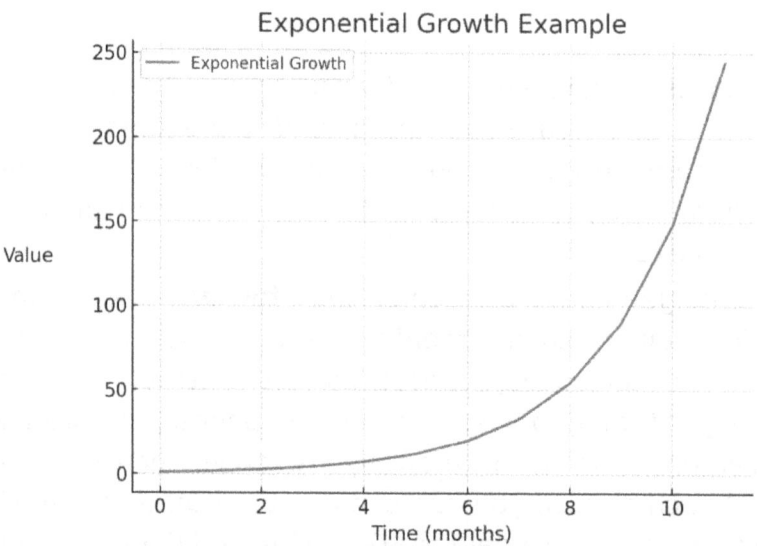

In charts, exponential growth appears as a curve that starts slowly and then bends sharply upward. The steepness of the curve depends on the growth factor: larger multipliers create faster acceleration, while smaller multipliers produce gentler—but still accelerating—curves.

Exponential change is harder to grasp than linear change. Our intuition is shaped by steady and predictable increments, so we consistently underestimate how quickly exponential growth can escalate. At first, it looks almost flat, but given enough time, it suddenly takes off and produces results far larger than expected.

Consider a startup's user growth that doubles monthly:

Month 1: 100 users (seems small)

Month 2: 200 users (still modest)

Month 3: 400 users (getting noticed)

Month 4: 800 users (solid growth)

Month 5: 1,600 users (impressive!)

Month 6: 3,200 users (wow!)

Month 12: 409,600 users (explosive!)

To the casual observer, it might seem like "nothing happened for months, then suddenly they exploded in month 12." In reality, the exponential growth was compounding all along. It just took time for the compounding to become visually dramatic.

Common exponential patterns often appear in business. Network effects are a classic case: platforms such as social media networks, online marketplaces, and communication tools grow exponentially because every new user increases the value for those already on the platform. Viral growth is another driver, where content, apps, or products spread rapidly through word-of-mouth and sharing, leading to sudden spikes in adoption.

Exponential change also shows up in compounding returns, whether in investment growth, improvements in customer lifetime value, or the accumulation of skills over time. Finally, market penetration can follow an exponential curve as new technologies or business models break through adoption barriers, reach tipping points, and accelerate rapidly.

Other examples of exponential change include:
- Book sales that double each month (10 → 20 → 40 → 80 → 160...).
- Views of a viral video multiply by 1.5x daily.
- Credit card debt compounding at 8% annually.

The danger of misreading change patterns

One of the most common mistakes in business is underestimating exponential threats. Competitors experiencing exponential growth may appear small and irrelevant in their early stages, only to suddenly dominate the market once growth accelerates. Kodak famously dismissed digital photography because the early numbers looked insignificant compared to its film business—until exponential adoption overwhelmed them.

At the same time, leaders often overestimate linear projections. Assuming current trends will continue in a straight line can blind decision-makers to looming shifts. Traditional retailers, for instance, projected steady linear growth for years and failed to anticipate the exponential rise of e-commerce, which fundamentally reshaped consumer behavior.

Planning failures also arise when companies prepare for linear growth while facing exponential demand. Budgeting with a linear mindset often leads to resource shortages. Many tech companies have discovered too late that their infrastructure could not scale quickly enough to keep up with exponential user adoption.

Another danger is missing the power of compounding effects. Small, consistent improvements can compound exponentially over time. A 1% daily improvement, for example, yields thirty-seven times growth over a year. Because this acceleration is invisible in the early stages, organizations frequently overlook its long-term impact.

Consequently, recognizing exponential patterns can mean the difference between catching a trend early and being blindsided by it. Companies that identified the exponential potential of mobile computing, social media, or cloud services early gained massive competitive advantages. Those who misread these patterns as linear trends were disrupted.

One way is to distinguish percentage changes from absolute changes. Linear growth adds the same fixed amount each period—for example, an extra $10,000 in revenue per month—while exponential growth multiplies by a percentage, such as 20% month over month.

It's also important to look for signs of compounding. If current results build upon previous results, and if each improvement makes future improvements easier, that is a strong indicator of exponential growth. Similarly, small numbers in early stages should not be dismissed if they are growing at high percentage rates. A company with just 100 users growing 10% each month could become tomorrow's dominant platform.

Finally, consider the underlying mechanics driving the change. Systems powered by network effects, viral sharing mechanisms, or compounding improvements often have exponential potential. Recognizing these forces early can help businesses prepare for rapid shifts before they become disruptive.

Remember, when you encounter data showing change over time, ask yourself:

- Is this adding the same amount each period (linear) or multiplying by a consistent factor (exponential)?
- What underlying mechanisms are driving this change?
- If this pattern continues, what will the numbers look like in 6 months or 2 years' time?

• Am I being deceived by the apparently "slow" start of what might be exponential growth?

Key takeaways

• Variables are the foundation of data. Knowing whether they are independent or dependent, continuous or categorical, shapes how you analyze, test, and visualize.

• Correlation is not causation. Strong stories treat correlations as clues, not conclusions. It's important to look beyond the surface.

• Sample size and representativeness are essential. A small or skewed dataset can produce confident but false narratives.

• Time frames shape perception. Avoid cherry-picking and present trends in full context.

• Linear and exponential growth tell very different stories. Misreading these patterns can lead to blind spots or strategic failure.

5

STORYTELLING

Before we dive into graphs, slide layouts, or color palettes, we first need to understand the foundation of impactful communication: storytelling.

We've all sat through presentations that overflowed with charts but that failed to engage us. The problem isn't the data. The problem is the lack of an overall narrative. Without a narrative structure, even the most insightful data can fail to connect, persuade, or inspire. That's why every great data communicator must also be a great storyteller.

The role of an effective storyteller is to:

1. Translate complexity into clarity.

2. Connect the abstract to the concrete.

3. Help people understand what the data means and why it matters.

1. Translate complexity into clarity

Data is rarely simple. You might be dealing with hundreds of thousands of rows, dozens of metrics, and multiple variables. A skilled storyteller takes what is messy and overwhelming and reshapes it into something that feels simple, direct, and digestible. Think of it as translating from "data-speak" into plain language, so the meaning is obvious at a glance.

2. Connect abstract numbers to concrete meaning

Numbers alone can feel distant. Saying that "churn fell by 4%" is abstract and might not land. But if you translate it into something concrete, like "that's the equivalent of 2,000 more customers staying with us this quarter," the audience suddenly understands the impact. By grounding abstract statistics in real-world meaning such as people, dollars, and time saved, you help your audience see what the numbers represent in their world.

3. Show people not just what the data says, but why it matters

Perhaps the most important role of the storyteller is connecting data to action. A chart can show sales rising or falling, but unless you explain why that matters to the organization's goals, to strategy, or to people's daily work, the insight won't stick. Great storytellers highlight the stakes: what's at risk, what's possible, what should be done next.

What is a story?

At its core, a story is a structured way of making sense of the world. It has a beginning, a middle, and an end. It introduces a situation, presents a challenge or conflict, and then resolves it. This pattern of setup, tension, and resolution can be seen everywhere from Shakespeare's plays to Netflix thrillers, TED talks, and even effective boardroom presentations.

Storytelling, of course, has been central to human experience for tens of thousands of years, from the Palawa oral traditions of the Tasmanian Aboriginals to the Chauvet cave drawings in Southern France. Our brains evolved to survive through stories. We passed on knowledge about danger, opportunity, and social norms through narratives, and this instinct still carries through to this day.

In fact, the famous experiment by cognitive psychologist Jerome Bruner found that people were 22 times more likely to remember a fact when it was wrapped in a story than when it was presented in isolation. This is because when we hear a story, we simulate the experience in our own minds, we relate emotionally, and we remember more. So if your data presentation isn't landing, don't add another chart. Add a story!

As Steve Jobs remarked in a 1994 interview, "The most powerful person in the world is the storyteller. The storyteller sets the vision, values, and agenda of an entire generation that is to come."

Storytelling vs. reporting

It's easy to treat data communication as a form of reporting where you dump all the available facts on your audience and expect them to figure out what's important. But this is a mistake. Always remember: reporting is passive, storytelling is active.

Reporting says: "Here's everything we know."

Storytelling says: "Here's what you need to know, and here's what it means."

What sets storytelling apart is editorial judgment. Storytellers don't just share everything—they curate. They emphasize what matters most, leave out what doesn't, and arrange the sequence so their audience is guided toward understanding.

In a report, you show a table of every product's performance. In a story, you highlight the outlier in the form of one product that suddenly surged after a pricing change and explain why it matters.

Reporting style	Storytelling style
Website traffic increased 18% in Q1	Our traffic turned a corner in January. After six months of stagnation, a single campaign drove a wave of new visitors—particularly on mobile. It wasn't just a bump, it was the start of a new trend.
Survey response rate was 65%	Nearly two-thirds of our customers took the time to share feedback, a strong signal that they're engaged and eager for their voices to shape our next steps.
Employee satisfaction score rose from 72 to 80 this year	Last year, employee satisfaction lagged at 72, but after rolling out flexible work options and mentorship programs, the score climbed to 80. It's a sign that investing in people directly translates into stronger morale and engagement.

The structure of a good story

Every data story needs a structure. Without it, even powerful insights feel scattered and unconvincing. Structure turns raw data into a journey your audience can follow. Think of a good narrative like a path through the forest. It doesn't just drop people into the middle of the trees and leave them to wander. It guides them, step by step, toward a destination. In the context of data, that destination is understanding, and ideally, action.

But how do you build a narrative from numbers?

You start with something familiar: the basic storytelling arc. This is the same structure found in novels, films, and speeches, and it works perfectly for data storytelling too.

The basic structure of a story consists of these three parts:

1. Setup: What's the context or current status quo?

2. Tension: What problem, anomaly, trend, or change has occurred to disrupt the status quo?

3. Resolution: What do we now know from the data? What should we do about it?

This three-part structure is simple but powerful. It creates anticipation and guides attention. It also prepares your audience to care about what you've discovered.

In a data story, the "setup" could be a baseline or historical trend. The "tension" could be a drop in revenue, a spike in customer churn, or a surprising correlation between weather patterns and product sales. Thirdly, the "resolution" is the insight you draw and the action you recommend.

Let's look at the following example of a three-part structure in action.

1. Setup: Over the past year, our email open rates have been consistent at around 22%.

2. Tension: But in the last two months, that number has dropped to 14%.

3. Resolution: A/B testing reveals subject line fatigue. Switching to a new headline theme based on a hot industry trend increased open rates by 30%. We recommend refreshing the content calendar to include more trending topics within our industry.

As you can see, by framing the data as a story with a clear beginning, middle, and end, the information is transformed into a narrative that people can follow, remember, and act upon. They won't just remember that "open rates dropped," they'll remember why it mattered and what to do next.

Let's now look at a second example:

1. Setup: For the past year, customer satisfaction has held steady at 89%.

2. Tension: But in the last quarter, we've seen a significant drop to 76%, driven mostly by mobile app users.

3. Resolution: Analysis of support tickets shows a spike in complaints after our most recent update. We recommend rolling back two features and launching a usability survey to prevent further churn.

This second data story concludes that customer satisfaction is fragile, especially when product updates disrupt established user habits. The numbers highlight where the problem emerged, and the analysis pinpoints what needs to change. By acting on these insights (rolling back features and engaging users through a survey), the company can restore trust, strengthen loyalty, and prevent further customer churn.

Both examples go beyond the raw numbers by instilling logic and structure to form a clear narrative that can be easily comprehended and remembered.

Using the same three-part storytelling structure, there are various types of data narratives we can use. Here are five common ones.

1. The change story: Something used to be one way, and now it's another.

Example: Infection rates stayed low for months, but then surged rapidly during the winter wave.

Why it works: By showing contrast, you can create instant relevance and urgency.

2. The comparison story: This group performed better than that group (e.g., market performance, A/B test results).

Example: Users acquired through referrals spent 40% more than those acquired through paid ads.

Why it works: Comparison stories fuel decision-making by making differences clear. Audiences naturally want to know what's better, faster, cheaper, or more effective.

3. The drill-down story: We found something interesting and went deeper to explain why (e.g., segmentation, root cause analysis).

Example: Sales dipped 8%, and a closer look showed the decline came almost entirely from first-time buyers.

Why it works: Drill-down stories mirror the process of discovery, taking the audience on a journey from "what happened" to "why it happened."

4. The outlier story: Something unexpected happened, and it matters (e.g., anomalies, surprises).

Example: One region outperformed all others, doubling revenue despite flat results elsewhere.

Why it works: Outliers disrupt expectations, and disruption demands attention. By spotlighting an anomaly, you challenge assumptions and invite new ways of thinking.

5. The performance story: Here's how we're tracking against a goal (e.g., KPIs, forecasts).

Example: We're at 72% of our annual revenue target with two months left in the year.

Why it works: Organizations are goal-driven, so performance stories provide clarity on whether efforts are on track or off course, and they create a natural call to action.

Each of these narrative forms is compatible with the same core principles of setup, tension, and resolution, but they differ in tone, emotional pull, and strategic purpose. Change stories stir urgency, comparison stories sharpen choices, drill-down stories spark curiosity, outlier stories capture surprise, and performance stories drive accountability. Choosing the right one will depend on what your audience needs to understand and why, as explored in Chapter 2.

Data as characters, plot & setting

Stories stick with people because they have shape, context, and emotion, which are all qualities that raw data often lacks. To transform numbers into narratives, it helps to borrow storytelling techniques from fiction writing. Just like a novel needs characters, a setting, and a plot, your data stories become more engaging when you give them these same three elements.

Characters are the subjects of your data—the people, products, teams, or markets the numbers represent. Think of them as your protagonists. When you say "customer churn increased," the character is the customer. When you say "sales in Region A outpaced Region B," the characters are those regions. Naming the characters gives the audience someone or something to care about.

Setting provides the environment for your data. This could be a time frame (last quarter, over five years), a place (Asia-Pacific, rural towns, online vs. offline), or a circumstance (holiday season, product launch, economic downturn). Setting turns data from abstract numbers into a lived context. For example, saying "sales dropped 12%" is one thing, but saying "sales dropped 12% during the normally busy holiday period" makes the same number far more meaningful.

Plot is the change over time—the movement that makes the story worth telling. A good plot shows tension and resolution: something unexpected happens, and we seek to understand why. This could be a sudden spike in app downloads, a steady decline in employee engagement scores, or a one-time surge in demand after a viral TikTok. Plot is what transforms a data point into a story arc.

When these three elements work together, data comes alive. Instead of writing "Our churn rate decreased 5%," you might say "After months of frustration with long wait times, customers finally saw relief in February when our support team doubled in size. Churn fell by 5% as a reflection of trust being rebuilt." By adding characters with motivations, settings that frame the stakes, and plots that show cause and effect, you create stories that people remember and act on.

Crafting hooks

Every story needs a way in, and in data storytelling, that entry point is the hook. Hooks can be woven into many parts of your communication, including your slide titles, your presentation title, or even the way you open verbally when you begin presenting.

Think of the hook as bait for your narrative: it gives people a reason to listen and a preview of where the story will take them. Done well, the hook acts as a promise. It tells the audience they won't just see numbers, they'll receive an answer, and once that promise is made, the rest of the story can deliver on it.

Hooks matter because audiences are busy, distracted, and oftentimes skeptical. Data can feel abstract or overwhelming if presented cold, but a strong opening signals why the information matters and why it's worth paying attention to. A good hook can also highlight the stakes, frame the surprise, or simply make the subject more relatable. It's the difference between saying "We analyzed customer churn" and saying "One in three new customers is leaving within the first month and here's why that matters."

Creating an effective hook doesn't mean forcing drama into the data. It just means framing the story with intention. This could be opening the presentation with the most compelling angle, whether that's a sharp contrast or an unexpected finding. To achieve this, you need to ask yourself: what's the question my audience already cares about, and how does this data help answer it?

As an example, I recently gave my team a talk on writing more effective weekly reports for upper management. Since most team members dread filing them on a Friday afternoon, internal reports often end up rushed and shallow. Unfortunately, this habit shows up later in performance reviews. My team excels at tallying outputs and raw data, but they struggle to explain the true value of their contributions or how their work supports the department's strategic direction. That's why my manager asked me to help them understand how to write stronger reports that showcase impact, not just activity.

I knew the topic of this presentation wouldn't excite my team, so I led with a hook. Within the first 10 seconds of my presentation, I acknowledged that weekly reporting is unpopular but promised that the same writing principles used for weekly report writing would help them write a more compelling self-performance review at the end of the year. This, in turn, impacts their chances of a promotion and a performance bonus. Suddenly, I had their undivided attention.

The key was that my hook tapped into their deeper motivation. Once they understood how the presentation could benefit them personally, they wanted to listen and take note.

The formula for a good hook

The most effective hooks generally share three key qualities: they are relevant, they carry specificity (often through a number), and they stir emotion. A line such as "7 out of 10 startups fail within their first 18 months" works because it is concrete, useful, and immediately strikes a nerve with anyone who has wrestled with the uncertainty of starting a business.

This hook also sparks curiosity by raising the question of why 7 out of 10 startups fail. When a reader encounters a line that asks why such a staggering failure rate exists, they instinctively want an explanation. Hooks like this are powerful because they leverage the human need to resolve uncertainty.

A good hook doesn't need to be hyperbole, though. Consider how online content is often packaged. A YouTube video titled "How to make $10,000 a year from data memes" may pull in viewers with its bold promise, but it also raises doubts.

Many readers will suspect exaggeration or clickbait. The result is that even if the headline produces clicks, it will struggle to build trust.

A subtler approach is often stronger. A headline like "Why experts think data memes will eat the Internet in 2026" or "Why so many people are sleeping on the data meme gravy train" creates intrigue without making an inflated promise. Both headlines signal something big is happening but leave space for the audience to connect the dots. If data memes are about to dominate, and if most people have overlooked the trend, then an opportunity exists. The hook works because it suggests value without directly spelling it out.

Another popular type of hook is a time-sensitive opportunity. For instance, one of the most popular hooks in the marketing world is the claim that we are "living in a unique moment in history." This framing plays on urgency and fear of missing out. The idea is that the present moment is special and fleeting, and unless you act now—whether by buying a course, investing in a business, or subscribing to content—you'll lose the chance forever. By tying the offer to a once-in-a-lifetime opportunity, marketers raise the stakes and push the audience toward immediate action.

Next, a strong hook should also leave the audience asking for more. For example, saying "I have inside news from a factory in China about a brand-new Apple product" instantly leaves people wanting to learn more about the product and what it could be. The word "inside news" stirs curiosity, while the mention of a secretive source adds intrigue about the product and how the information was obtained.

Now contrast this with a weak hook. A poor storyteller will open their story with a line like, "That reminds me of the time…" or "I can't remember if I told you, but I once…" These openings fail on several levels. First, they don't signal any clear payoff for listening—will the audience learn something, be entertained, or gain a new perspective? The answer isn't clear. Second, the storyteller hasn't established why the story matters to the audience. On both fronts, this type of hook fails to stimulate any curiosity in the audience.

The same principle applies to data storytelling. A weak hook might begin with, "Here are the latest numbers from last quarter." This is flat and gives the audience no reason to care. A stronger alternative would be, "Last quarter's numbers reveal a surprising shift in customer behavior that could change how we prioritize marketing spend." This phrasing not only signals value regarding how marketing spend is prioritized but also adds that there is something surprising to be shared.

Another example could be, "Buried in the sales data is a trend that explains why one competitor is pulling ahead—and what we can do about it." Again, this example creates anticipation and gives the audience a reason to listen.

In the end, bold hooks may generate attention, but hooks that combine relevance, intrigue, and implied value do more. They capture interest in the moment and also earn the trust that keeps audiences engaged.

Guiding the narrative

Transitions are often the invisible glue of a good story, yet they're one of the commonly overlooked elements in data storytelling. Moving from one chart to the next is like shifting scenes in a film. If you don't guide the audience gracefully through those shifts, they can lose track of the narrative. That's why it helps to use signposts: remind them what they just saw, explain what they're about to see, and connect the dots by explaining why it matters. These small moments of orientation act like anchors, keeping people grounded and attentive even as the story moves forward.

Matthew Dicks, an award-winning storyteller and author, often emphasizes the importance of these connective tissues in keeping a narrative alive. A useful technique here is the "but/therefore" rule, popularized by the creators of *South Park*. Instead of linking ideas with "and then," which flattens momentum, they suggest using "but" and "therefore" to create tension and causality.

The same approach works in data storytelling. "But" highlights a shift, obstacle, or contradiction in the data, and "therefore" signals consequence, insight, or resolution. Together, they mimic the natural rhythm of setup, tension, and resolution used in data storytelling.

Example 1

Our sales rose 20% last quarter, **but** most of the growth came from a single region, which makes us vulnerable if that market slows. **Therefore**, we need to diversify our growth by investing in underperforming regions.

Example 2

Customer satisfaction scores have improved steadily over the past year, **but** churn has not decreased. **Therefore**, the issue isn't satisfaction with the product—it's pricing, and that's where we need to focus.

Repetition also plays a similar role in driving the narrative and strengthening the message. It's easy to assume that once you've said something, it has landed. But in reality, people miss details, get distracted, or need reinforcement for an idea to truly stick. A core insight mentioned once on slide three should resurface on slide ten and return again at the end. Far from being redundant, this rhythm of repetition helps embed the takeaway in memory, making it more likely that your audience carries it with them.

Next, a strong story needs a strong and deliberate ending. Too often, presentations fizzle out with a final chart or an open-ended "any questions?" Instead, think of the ending as landing a plane. Restate the key finding. Clarify the decision or action that should follow. Remind your audience of why it matters and what they should do with the information. That final moment shapes what lingers in their minds after the meeting ends.

Lastly, good narratives create space for questions. Don't be afraid to leave your audience thinking. "Here's what we know, and here's what we're watching next" is a perfectly valid resolution. Curiosity is contagious, and if your story starts the next stage of exploration, that can lead to a future win.

In the next chapter, we'll explore the visual language of data and how choosing the right chart can either reinforce your insight or bury it under confusion.

Key takeaways

- A story has three parts: setup, tension, and resolution. Use this structure in data storytelling.
- Storytelling is not reporting. Curate and highlight what matters.
- By treating data elements like characters, setting, and plot, you can pick out the story more easily.
- Strong hooks—specific, emotional, and relevant—capture attention and inspire curiosity.
- Transitions, repetition, and a clear ending solidify understanding and make the story memorable.

6

VISUALIZING DATA

Raw data, in its natural form, is abstract. A table of numbers may hold valuable insights, but on its own, it rarely speaks to us. Our brains aren't designed to scan endless rows and columns, searching for patterns. Instead, we are wired to detect shapes, contrasts, trends, and movement. These visual cues instantly tell us when something stands out or changes.

That is the power of a good chart. It transforms numbers into something we can see—a story the brain can recognize at a glance. Visualization bridges the gap between raw information and human understanding, turning complexity into clarity. The first decision, though, is what type of chart should you use?

Different visuals answer different questions. Line charts show trends over time. Bar charts compare quantities. Scatterplots reveal relationships. Pie charts work only when categories are few and differences are large enough to see. Otherwise, they mislead. Knowing these various strengths and weaknesses of each type of visualization will help you match your data to the right chart.

Tables

Tables are useful when the exact number matters (say, in financial reporting or reference material), but, as storytelling devices, they deliver precision at the expense of clarity. Ultimately, a table requires work. The audience has to scan, compare, and mentally calculate what the story is. That effort means the narrative risks getting lost. In live presentations, tables are best used as backup material rather than as the main visual.

Country Sales And Ad Spend (2015-2025)

	Country	Year	Sales (in $M)	Ad Spend (in $M)
1	USA	2015	783	114
2	USA	2016	787	114
3	USA	2017	808	115
4	USA	2018	845	130
5	USA	2019	801	136

Best suited for: raw or precise numerical data like financial statements, reference lookups, or datasets where the exact figure is more important than the trend.

Bar charts

Bar charts are perfect for making comparisons. They are easy to read and work well for ranking products, measuring costs by team, or comparing survey results across regions.

There are three common types of bar charts. Vertical bar charts are the most common, especially when order or time matters, as they make it easy to see progressions such as sales over months or years. Horizontal bar charts, meanwhile, are more effective when category names are long, since the labels fit neatly along the side.

Lastly, stacked or grouped bar charts add another layer of detail by showing comparisons within categories, such as breaking down sales by both channel and region. If you are comparing total sales across five countries, you can use a standard bar chart. But if you also want to show how much of those sales came from digital versus traditional channels, a stacked bar chart lets you display both the overall total and the breakdown within each bar. While these charts can reveal more nuance, using too many comparisons at once can overwhelm the viewer.

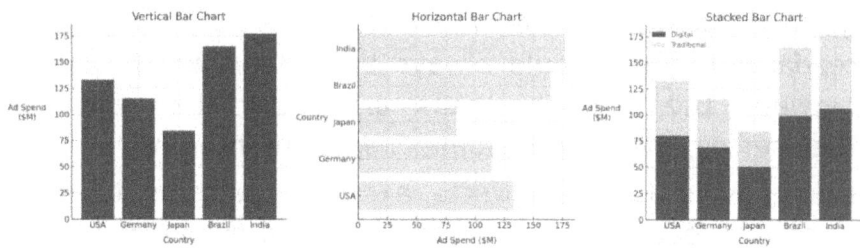

For all three types of bar charts, it's best to limit the number of bars to 10 or fewer. To focus attention, you can highlight one bar in a bold color while keeping the others in muted tones for context. You can also add data labels to the ends of bars or annotate key differences (e.g., "+25% vs. last year") to reduce cognitive load and highlight key messages.

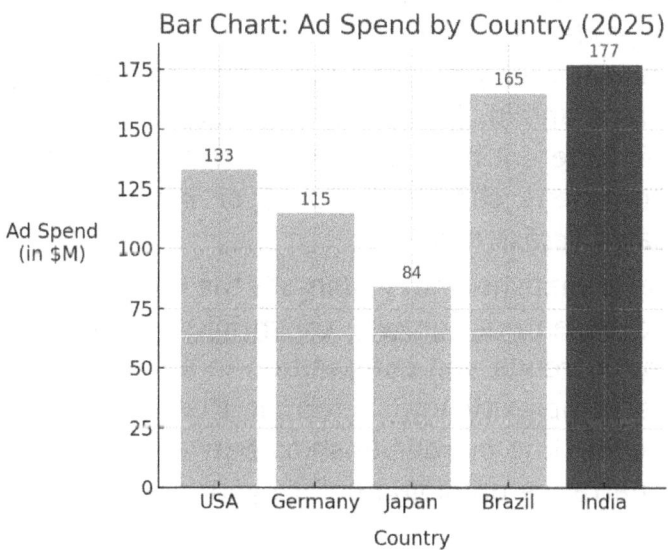

For bar charts, always start the axis at zero to avoid distortion. Keep bar widths consistent and spacing narrower than bar width to ensure readability. Starting at zero is important because bar lengths represent actual values. If the axis began at some higher number, the bars would look much shorter or taller than they really are, which could mislead the viewer. The width of the bars is flexible, but for readability, they should always be wider than the spaces between them. If the gaps are wider than the bars themselves, the chart becomes harder to interpret.

Lastly, avoid using 3D effects, excessive patterns, textures, or an overload of bright colors that could distort perception and reduce clarity.

Best suited for: categorical or discrete data like sales by product, expenses by department, or survey responses by demographic group.

Bar Chart Races

Bar chart races are a dynamic variation of the bar chart designed to show how rankings change over time. These visuals have exploded in popularity as they turn dry tables into dynamic narratives: you don't just see who's leading, you watch the race unfold. Popular bar chart races on social media show how different brands gain or lose market share, how cities' populations change in rank, or how products contribute to sales across quarters.

Instead of a static snapshot, they animate the movement of bars as new data enters, grows, or shrinks, letting the audience see both trends and competition in a single view. This condenses complexity into a format that feels alive, where change over time or relationships between variables play out like a narrative unfolding before your eyes.

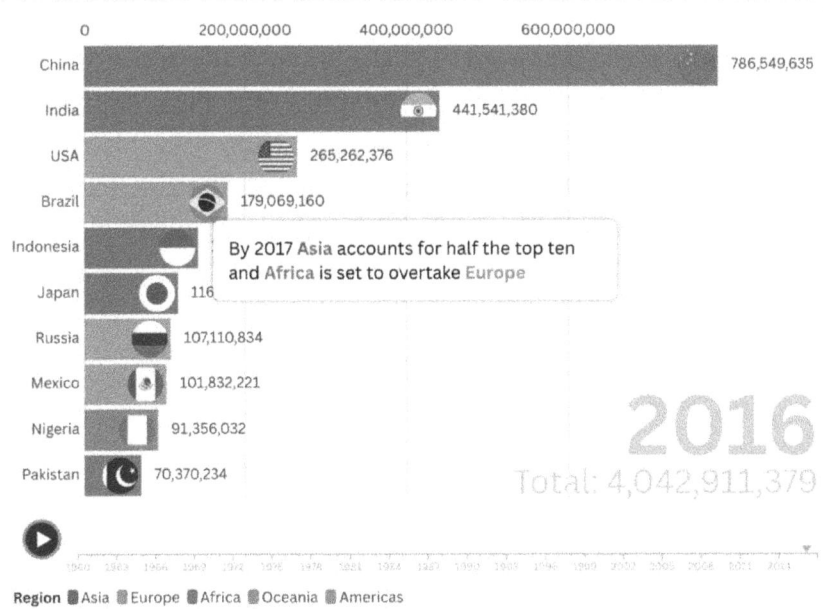

Design and restraint are crucial when it comes to designing a good bar chart race. Too many bars on the screen at once overwhelms the viewer, so limiting the display to the top 5–10 categories keeps the story engaging. Axis scales must remain consistent across frames, or the animation risks being misleading. And while animation draws attention, it should not run so fast that viewers cannot process the movement.

Bar chart races are best used for competitive stories where the audience needs to see shifts in ranking and momentum. They work especially well in presentations or social media videos but are less suited for static reports, where the story is lost without motion.

Best suited for: time-based rankings, such as top-performing products, fastest-growing companies, or shifting market leaders.

Histograms

Histograms are designed to show the distribution of a continuous variable by grouping data into bins (intervals). Unlike bar charts, which compare categories, histograms reveal the shape and distribution of data. They're especially useful for spotting patterns such as skewness, peaks, gaps, or outliers.

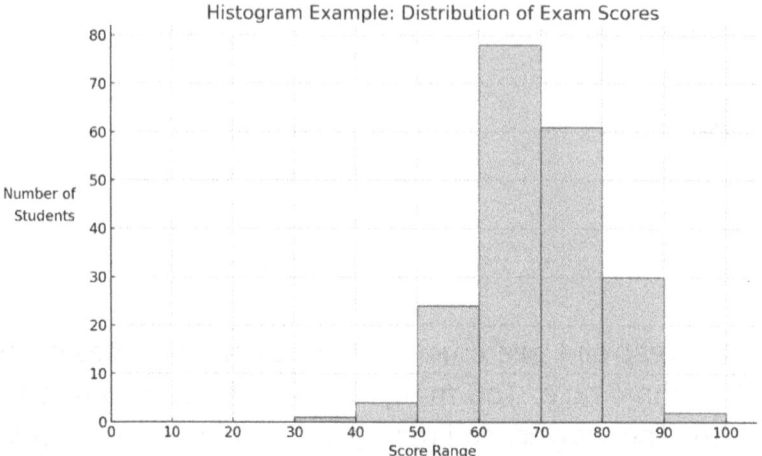

For example, the histogram above shows the distribution of exam scores for 100 students. Each bar represents the number of students whose scores fall within a specific range (e.g., 60–70, 70–80, etc.). This makes it easy to see where most students scored, whether the distribution is centered around a particular point, and how spread out the results are.

As with bar charts, the x- and y-axes should begin at 0 whenever possible to avoid exaggerating differences unless the data naturally requires a different scale (i.e., temperature ranges). However, unlike a bar chart, there shouldn't be any white space between the bars. This reflects the fact that the bars represent ranges on a continuous scale rather than being separate categories.

Histograms are best suited for numerical data where the goal is to understand frequency distribution.

Best suited for: continuous numerical data, such as test scores, customer ages, product prices, or time durations.

Line charts

Line charts are the clearest way to show change over time. They transform rows of dates and numbers into an immediate sense of direction: rising, falling, or flatlining. Line charts also show how quickly it happened. Was the increase steady and predictable (linear), or sudden and dramatic (logarithmic)? This sense of movement is why line charts are often the backbone of trend analysis and forecasting.

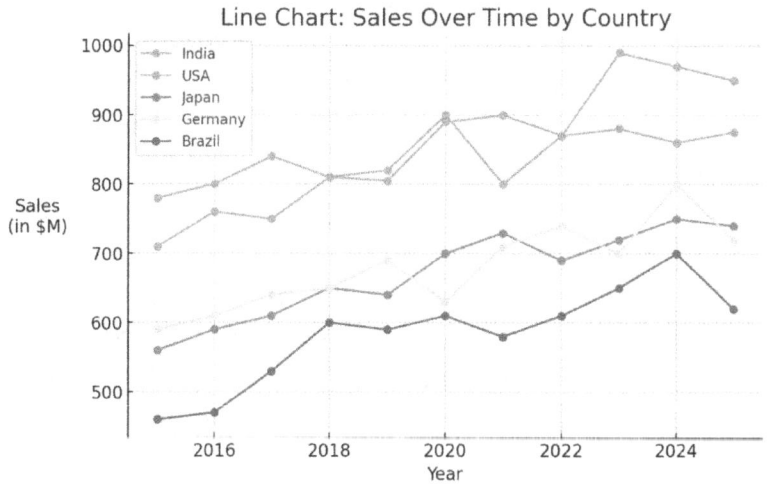

Placing time on the x-axis allows the eye to move from left to right in the way we naturally read progressions—past to present, or present to future. The vertical (y) axis then represents the variable being measured, so the rise and fall of the line directly reflects how that value changes across time. If the axes are reversed, the story becomes harder to follow as it forces the viewer to interpret trends in an unfamiliar direction.

In addition, make sure the intervals on the x-axis are consistent (such as equal spacing for months or years), since irregular spacing can easily distort how viewers perceive the trend. Note that the axis does not need to start at zero like it does with a bar chart, because in a line chart, the focus is on how values change over time. Starting the axis closer to the data makes it easier to see the ups and downs clearly.

Next, limit the number of lines. More than 3–4 lines can get messy. Always label lines directly, if possible, instead of relying on a legend, which is harder to navigate. You can also highlight key points (peaks, troughs, turning points) to guide the audience's attention to what matters most (instead of leaving the reader to find them), but use them sparingly.

Another way to direct the audience's attention is to use muted colors plus one bold highlight. By keeping most lines in muted, neutral tones and making just one line bold (e.g., a strong color or heavier weight), you signal which line is the focus of the story. If all lines are bright and bold, the viewer doesn't know where to look first.

If your data story is about the Indian market, for example, you can use this color technique to highlight its growth history while still allowing the audience to see how India's performance fits within the broader global picture.

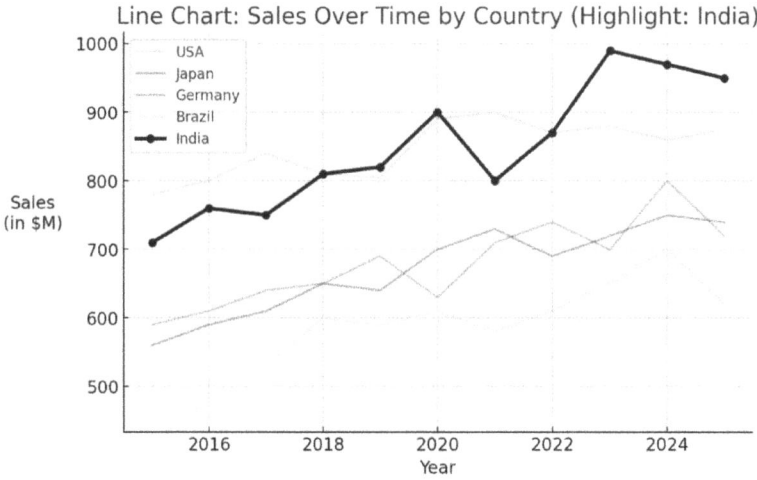

As you can see, this version of the chart is designed to guide the viewer's attention toward India. By showing the other countries in softer, pastel tones and highlighting India in a bold color, the chart makes it immediately clear where the focus lies. The supporting lines provide necessary context, but they don't compete for attention.

Best suited for: data with a time dimension, such as monthly revenue, daily active users, stock prices, or long-term growth trends.

Scatterplots

Scatterplots are ideal for showing correlations, such as how ad spend correlates with sales. They let you explore whether two variables move together, like advertising spend and sales, or whether patterns emerge across clusters, like customer segments behaving differently. They're also great for spotting outliers that don't fit the general trend.

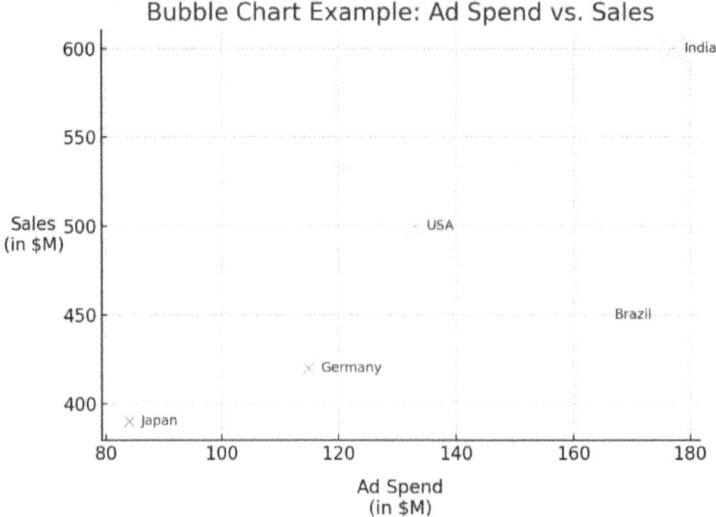

Note that scatterplots aren't limited to two variables. In a 3D scatterplot, a third axis is added so you can plot three variables at once, while in a 4D scatterplot, a fourth variable is usually represented through color or bubble size. Although this can reveal more complex relationships in a single view, interpretation quickly becomes difficult.

A flat 2D chart is straightforward, but 3D plots often require perspective or rotation to read properly, and 4D plots force the audience to decode multiple layers of meaning at once. As a result, these higher-dimensional scatterplots are best reserved for exploration, while simpler 2D versions usually serve storytelling more effectively.

To make scatterplots effective, both axes should be labeled clearly with units, and scales should remain consistent. If zero adds meaning to the story, it should be included; if not, the axis should be tailored to the relevant range of data.

Highlighting patterns can also strengthen the story. A regression line or trend line helps reveal whether the relationship is positive, negative, or weak, and annotations can guide the reader's eye to significant clusters or outliers.

While scatterplots can spark rich insights, they demand careful execution. Without clear labeling, thoughtful design, and contextual explanation, they risk confusing more than they clarify. They are most effective with audiences who are already comfortable interpreting data visualizations, and they benefit from a storyteller who can guide attention to the relationships that matter most.

Best suited for: paired numerical data, especially when testing relationships like marketing spend vs. conversions, education vs. income, or hours studied vs. exam scores.

Pie charts

Deceptively simple, pie charts look familiar and friendly, which is why they appear so often, but they rarely communicate well. Humans struggle to compare angles accurately, especially when slices are similar in size. A pie chart with five or six equal-looking slices often leaves the audience guessing instead of understanding. Alternatives such as stacked bars, 100% bars, or simply labeling percentages directly make proportions clearer and more memorable.

As a quick rule of thumb, use pie charts sparingly, and only when you have very few categories with starkly different shares.

In terms of design choices, keep the number of slices limited, order them logically (such as largest to smallest), and label them directly with values or percentages so the reader doesn't have to jump between the chart and a legend.

Lastly, try to use contrasting colors sparingly to highlight one important slice, but avoid rainbow palettes that create visual noise. Steer clear of 3D pies, which distort perception, and resist the temptation to "explode" every slice, which distracts more than it informs.

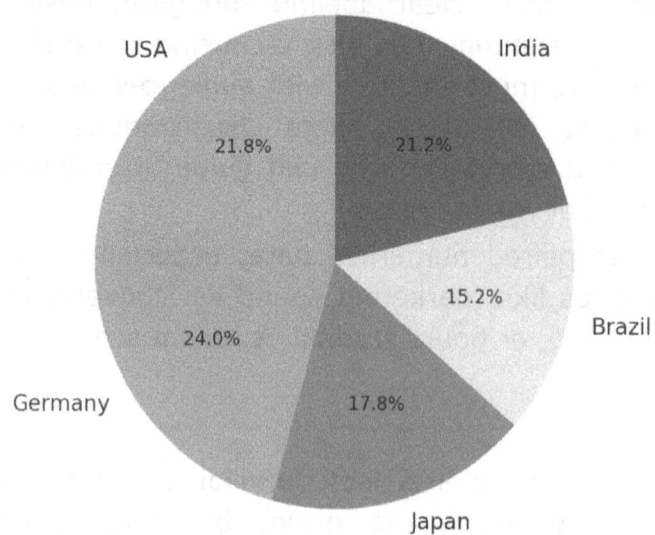

Best suited for: part-to-whole relationships, with no more than 3 categories, such as market share, budget allocation, or survey splits.

Heatmaps

Heatmaps are one of the most effective ways to reveal patterns, clusters, and outliers across large or complex datasets. By using color intensity to represent values, they allow the audience to instantly see where activity is concentrated, where it's sparse, and how clusters form. Instead of scanning rows of numbers in a table, your audience can spot "hot spots" and "cold spots" in a single glance. For example, a heat map can reveal which years generated the most product sales and which countries had the strongest sales.

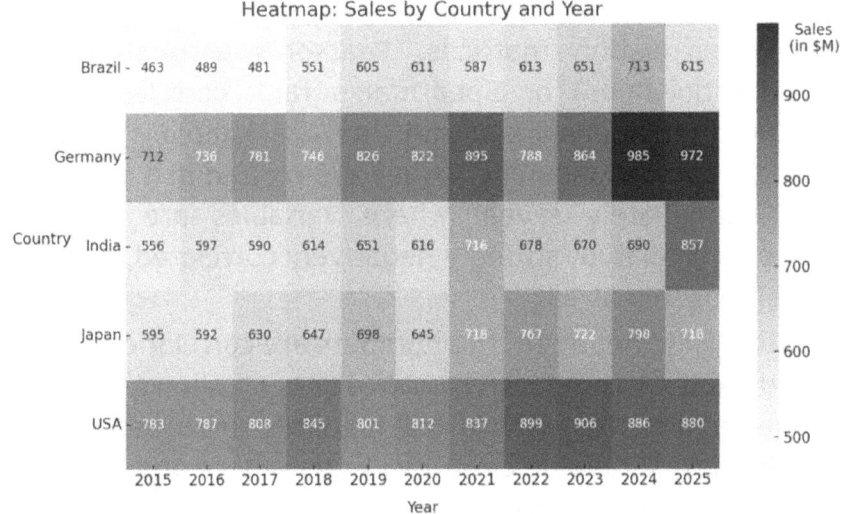

Heatmaps aren't limited to grids of data. They can also be geographic, showing activity by location. For instance, a heatmap of the United States Wind Turbine Database reveals major clusters of turbines across the central states, giving viewers immediate insight into regional energy production in the US.

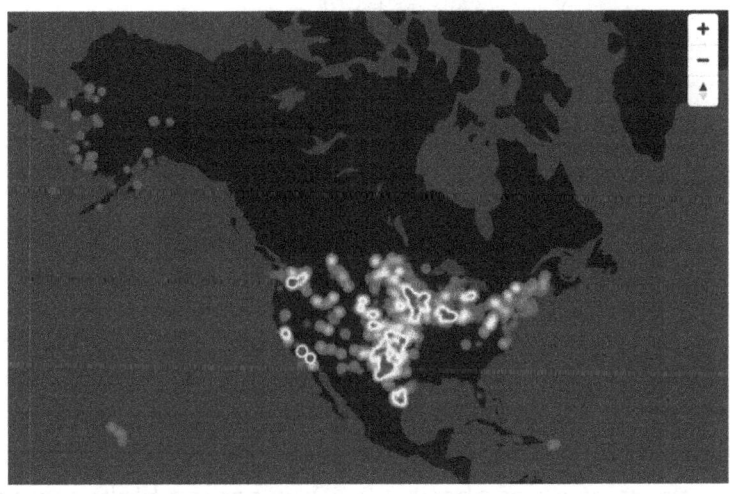

One of the more common use cases of heat maps is for showing correlation matrices. Pearson's correlation (for linear relationships) or Spearman's rank correlation (for monotonic relationships) can be calculated between variables, and the resulting values are plotted in a grid. The colors immediately reveal where variables are strongly positively correlated, strongly negatively correlated, or show little relationship at all.

In the following heatmap, the numbers are correlation scores ranging from −1 to +1. A value close to +1 shows a strong positive relationship, where one variable increases as the other increases. A value close to −1 shows a strong negative relationship, where one variable decreases as the other increases. A value near zero means there is little to no relationship between the two variables.

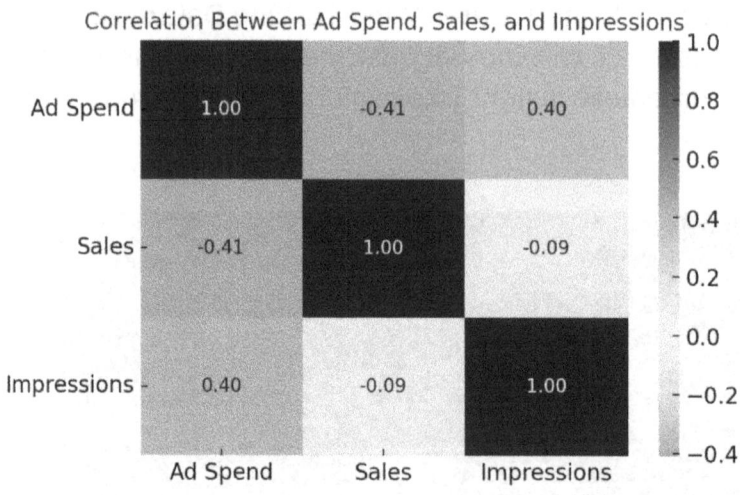

According to the heatmap, ad spend and sales have a correlation of −0.41, which suggests that as spending goes up, sales tend to move down. Ad spend and impressions show a correlation of about +0.40, meaning higher spending generally produces more impressions. Sales and impressions, however, are near zero at −0.09, which tells us they don't strongly move together in this dataset.

The colors reinforce these numbers. Red tones highlight negative correlations, blue tones highlight positive ones, and lighter shades around white show weak or no relationship. The diagonal values are always 1.00 because a variable is perfectly correlated with itself. Together, the numbers and the colors make it easy to spot which relationships are strong, which are weak, and which go in opposite directions.

As with all types of charts, design choices are key to readability. First, the choice of color palette has a big impact on how easily people can interpret a heat map. Different types of data call for different types of color scales and using the wrong one can distort the story. The three most common are sequential, diverging, and categorical palettes.

A sequential palette moves in one direction, usually from light to dark. It is best for data that progresses from low to high without a meaningful middle point. For example, you might use a light-to-dark blue scale to show website traffic by hour of the day—lighter shades for fewer visits, darker shades for heavier traffic. This makes it easy to see where activity peaks.

A diverging palette uses two contrasting colors that meet at a neutral midpoint. It is designed for data with a meaningful center, such as zero, an average, or a balance point. For example, in a correlation heat map, negative correlations could be shown in shades of blue, positive correlations in shades of red, and values near zero in white. This lets the viewer instantly see which variables move together, which move in opposite directions, and which are unrelated.

A categorical palette uses distinct, unrelated colors. Unlike sequential or diverging scales, there is no order to the colors—they are simply meant to differentiate between categories. For example, a map showing sales by region might assign green to North America, orange to Europe, purple to Asia, and so on. The goal is not to show magnitude but to clearly separate groups.

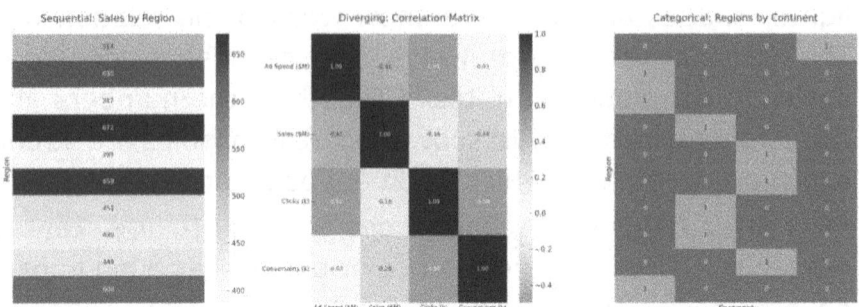

Keep in mind, too, that color perception is subjective, so without a clear legend, viewers may misinterpret intensity. Accessibility is another concern; colorblind-friendly palettes should be chosen to ensure all viewers can read the chart.

Best suited for: two-dimensional data with continuous or categorical axes—like time vs. day of week, product vs. region, or demographic group vs. behavior.

Beyond the common chart types discussed in this chapter, there are also specialty charts that can bring unique value when used in the right context. For example, a treemap can reveal how parts contribute to a whole across multiple levels of hierarchy—useful for showing the relative size of subcategories within a larger category, such as product lines within a business unit. A waterfall chart, on the other hand, is powerful for illustrating cumulative gains and losses, making it easy to see how individual factors add up to a final total.

That said, these charts come with a learning curve. If your audience is unfamiliar with the format, you'll need to spend time explaining how to read it before they can focus on the insight itself. In high-stakes presentations or fast-moving discussions, that extra effort can become a barrier rather than a benefit. The key is to balance novelty with clarity. A specialized chart can make your story more engaging and precise, but only if it doesn't slow your audience down. When in doubt, lean on simpler forms that your viewers already know how to interpret. Bar charts, line charts, and scatterplots often communicate just as effectively, without the risk of distraction.

Key takeaway
• The right chart type depends on the data—lines for trends, bars for comparisons, histograms for grouping data, scatterplots for relationships, heatmaps for patterns, and tables for precision.

7

DESIGN PRINCIPLES

Once you've selected the right chart type, the next question is how you design it.

However, great visual storytelling isn't about flashy tools or advanced software—it's about clarity. With purposeful design choices, even simple tools like Excel or Google Sheets can produce visuals that are powerful and persuasive.[1] And yet, too often, charts are designed and created without asking a critical question: *what do I want my audience to see first?* That's the heart of visual thinking. You're guiding attention. You're leading the eye from question to insight.

This is where the idea of visual hierarchy becomes essential. Visual hierarchy refers to what the audience sees first, second, third, and so forth. Every element on the screen, from axes to colors to labels, guides the eye and are either helping or hurting your message. That's why visual thinking requires intention with the goal of creating the most direct path from data to understanding.

Think of your chart like a movie scene. Where should your viewer look first? Where should they look next? What's the climax of this story? Your use of color, size, position, and whitespace can then be used to structure a story and create that journey. Each element can be used like a narrative device, guiding the audience through a beginning, middle, and end.

---

[1] Excel and Google Sheets are widely used and remain powerful starting points, though limited in interactivity compared to platforms like Tableau or Flourish.

This may mean breaking your data down across multiple charts and visualizations. Whereas a single complex chart can overwhelm, a sequence of simple visuals can build understanding step by step. This might entail leading with context, introducing the change or tension, and then showing resolution. In this way, each visual becomes a scene in a story, building toward the key message.

The first step is establishing context. A chart without a frame of reference is like a story without a setting. This is why it's important to start by showing the baseline—whether it's a long-term trend, an industry benchmark, or a historical average. This creates a sense of "normal" against which change can be understood.

Next comes contrast. Stories thrive on tension, and visuals can create it by revealing what disrupts the baseline. A sharp spike, a sudden dip, or a divergence between two lines builds curiosity and invites interpretation. This is the moment when your audience begins to lean in, asking "why?"

Then comes the climax of the story. This is where you direct attention to the key finding. Visual techniques like color emphasis, annotations, or overlays can highlight the driver of change or the turning point in the data. Without this moment of focus, your audience may see movement but miss meaning.

Finally, provide a resolution. A chart sequence that ends in mystery may intrigue, but a story that ends with clarity inspires action. This might mean showing how a corrective measure reversed the decline, projecting what will happen if the trend continues, or contrasting two possible futures. Resolution ensures the narrative doesn't just inform—it guides decisions.

This story arc can be applied across individual charts or a sequence of them. A presentation may begin with a broad overview, narrow to a disruptive insight, highlight the cause, and conclude with an actionable recommendation. Each chart becomes a chapter in the narrative, carefully ordered to build momentum and deliver impact.

Here's a practical example of different design principles in action, shown as a sequence of charts:

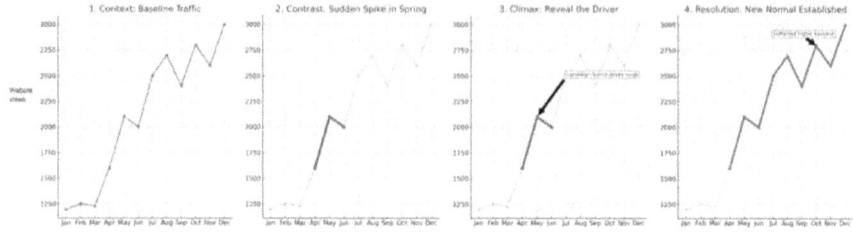

1. Context: The baseline trend in website traffic is established. The audience sees what "normal" looks like.

2. Contrast: A sudden spike in spring is highlighted in red, introducing tension and prompting curiosity.

3. Climax: An annotation reveals the driver of change: a campaign launch. The audience now understands why the spike occurred.

4. Resolution: The chart reframes the data to show a sustained new baseline (highlighted in blue), guiding the audience toward an actionable conclusion.

This sequence demonstrates how visual hierarchy and storytelling techniques (color, annotation, sequencing) transform raw numbers into a clear, memorable narrative rather than simply summarizing the data.

The power of simplicity

A common mistake is over-design, which is essentially an attempt to impress rather than express. Just because your charting tool can add gradients, drop shadows, and animations doesn't mean it should. In data storytelling, simplicity is your greatest asset. It creates clarity, builds trust, and drives action.

Assume your audience is busy and their attention is fragmented. They don't have time to untangle a messy chart or decode a wall of text. If they're confused, they'll disengage and any valuable insights that you have discovered will be lost. That's why your job as a storyteller isn't to showcase every chart, every variable, every angle.

Think about it like editing a film. The raw footage is necessary to make the movie, but it's not the movie. What ends up on screen is the version that best serves the story. That's your goal: to become an editor of your own analysis.

This begins with how you prepare your content. You might start with dozens of data points, but ask yourself: which one drives the story forward? What is the core insight? What action do I want someone to take? Once you know that, everything else becomes either supportive or expendable.

There's even a concept in design called signal-to-noise ratio. High signal, low noise. That's what you want in your data stories. More meaning, less mess. Every visual and every word should be in service of the signal. Once you know what information to focus on, you need to be ruthless about design and layout. If a chart element doesn't help the story, remove it. If a sentence doesn't add value, cut it. Every axis, label, title, and bullet point should earn its place. If it doesn't, it's clutter.

Next, whitespace will be one of your strongest tools. Whitespace—also called negative space—is the empty area around text, visuals, or chart elements. While it might seem like a waste of real estate, whitespace gives people's eyes room to breathe. It lets the important things stand out.

Here's a before-and-after example of whitespace in action.

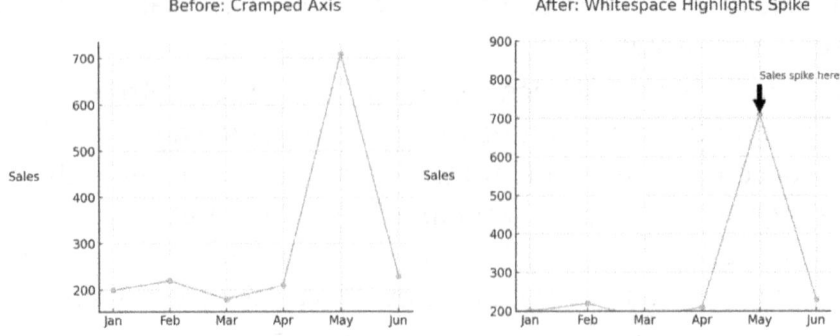

Before (left): The spike in May looks cramped against the chart's ceiling, making it harder to appreciate its significance.

After (right): By adding whitespace above the data and annotating the peak, the spike is framed more clearly and becomes the focal point of the story.

Note that whitespace doesn't have to be white; it can be any background color. That said, using a white or very light background is often recommended because it creates high contrast with text and visuals, improving readability and accessibility.

The next key aspect of simplicity is consistency. Use the same color scheme across slides. Align elements neatly. Stick to a small set of fonts and sizes. When your audience doesn't have to constantly adjust to new formats, they can focus on the content. Consistency reduces cognitive load and makes your message easier to absorb.

Simplifying also means anticipating confusion before it happens. Label your charts clearly. Avoid technical jargon unless your audience knows it. Acronyms or jargon like "GDP CAGR" can alienate people if left unexplained. If a term is important, define it. If a concept is complex, break it into parts.

It's worth noting that sometimes, a chart isn't the answer. In some cases, a single number, clearly presented in a bold font, tells the story best. For instance, "94% customer satisfaction" doesn't need a pie chart. It needs emphasis.

Of course, simplicity doesn't mean being shallow. You can deliver nuance and depth, just not all at once. You can layer your communication: lead with the insight, and offer detail in supporting slides, footnotes, or appendices. Let the audience dive deeper if they choose. Don't make them wade through everything to get to the point.

This approach builds trust. When you present your story in a simple, focused way, it signals that you respect the audience's time. It shows that you've done the hard thinking, so they don't have to, and that makes people far more likely to engage with your recommendations.

At the end of the day, visual thinking is about empathy. You're not building a chart for yourself. You're building it for someone who hasn't spent hours in the data. Your job is to make it obvious. Think of the most memorable presentations you've seen. The ones that stick usually aren't overloaded with detail. They're clean and focused, which is the power of simplicity.

Color

Color is often the strongest signal in any visualization. A single bold highlight in an otherwise muted palette can instantly call out the key data point, guiding the audience's eye to exactly where you want them to land.

While color provides visual appeal, an excessive number of colors can be overwhelming. Unless you need to visualize a high number of categories or data points, it's best to limit visualizations to seven colors or fewer for categorical distinction. This will also help to ensure your visualizations look professional. In addition, it's important to assign meaning to color—whether it's distinguishing categories or highlighting a single data point—while resisting the urge to use it as decoration.

If your organization has a set color palette for visual branding purposes, then it makes sense to start there, especially if your visualizations are to be viewed by customers and shared on social media. If you are choosing a palette, you can find free resources like Adobe Color CC (https://color.adobe.com/create/color-wheel) with an interactive color wheel to help you customize and select color combinations. It's important to pick distinctive colors, especially if you need to distinguish a large number of groups. It's also worth remembering that colors carry emotional associations. Bright pink and teal, for example, project a playful and youthful tone, which is why they appear in user trend charts for companies like Tinder and TikTok. Traditional blues, on the other hand, signal trust and professionalism, making them a staple for companies such as Microsoft and IBM. Red is often used for war data, danger, or losses in financial charts. Green is frequently tied to growth, money, or environmental topics. Orange conveys energy and urgency, making it effective in calls to action or highlighting warnings. Purple is commonly associated with creativity or luxury, while gray tones are best reserved for background context.

Lastly, you may need to pay attention to cultural contexts when designing and presenting your data. In East Asia, for example, red is associated with "good fortune" and "prosperity." Stock price gains are therefore displayed in red and falls in green. This is the opposite color scheme for stock price movements in the West, where green is associated with positive. Avoiding red and green to visualize gains and losses is one solution to neutralize potential confusion.

Accessibility

A truly effective data story is one that everyone in the audience can understand, including those with limited sight.

Around one in twelve men and one in two hundred women are colorblind, which means that a chart relying only on red and green to distinguish gains and losses may be unreadable for many. A better approach is to use contrast in multiple ways—pairing color with shape, pattern, or clear labels. A downward arrow communicates decline even if the color difference is missed, and strong textual labeling ensures no viewer is left guessing. Tools like ColorBrewer (http://colorbrewer2.org/) also provide a filter that lets you select from palettes pre-tested for color blindness.

Legibility is another cornerstone of accessibility. Charts that look sharp on a desktop monitor can quickly fall apart on a mobile device or projector screen. Also, fonts that are too small, labels that are crowded, and legends that require constant cross-checking all add unnecessary friction.

For online contexts, charts should be accompanied by alt text or descriptions that capture the key message. A bar chart showing sales growth, for example, might be described as "Quarterly sales increased steadily from Q1 to Q4, rising 35% overall." This ensures that the insight is available even to those using screen readers, and it also helps clarify the intended takeaway for everyone else.

Scale

Scale is one of the most powerful, but also the most easily abused tools in data visualization. Just as color can direct attention, scale determines the weight and meaning of data on the page. A larger element instantly reads as more important, while smaller elements fade into the background. Position reinforces this effect, since most audiences instinctively scan from left to right, top to bottom. Placing your most critical message in a prominent position, with an appropriate size, ensures it isn't overlooked. But with this power comes responsibility. Manipulated or misleading scales can distort reality and erode trust.

One of the most common pitfalls is the truncated axis, when a chart does not start at zero. A truncated y-axis can make tiny differences look dramatic, while stretching an axis can flatten a significant trend until it appears meaningless. A bar chart starting at 50 instead of 0 can make two values like 52 and 54 look drastically different, even though the actual gap is minimal. On the flip side, stretching an axis too wide can flatten a meaningful trend until it looks insignificant.

In some cases, truncation is legitimate (for example, when showing small changes in temperature). But more often, it exaggerates differences and erodes trust with your audience. As an example, imagine stock market fluctuations plotted on a chart where the y-axis begins at 10,000 instead of 0. A normal daily change of 15 points suddenly looks like a dramatic crash. The numbers haven't changed, only the scale. Without context, viewers may walk away with a false impression of crisis when, in reality, the market is behaving within expected volatility.

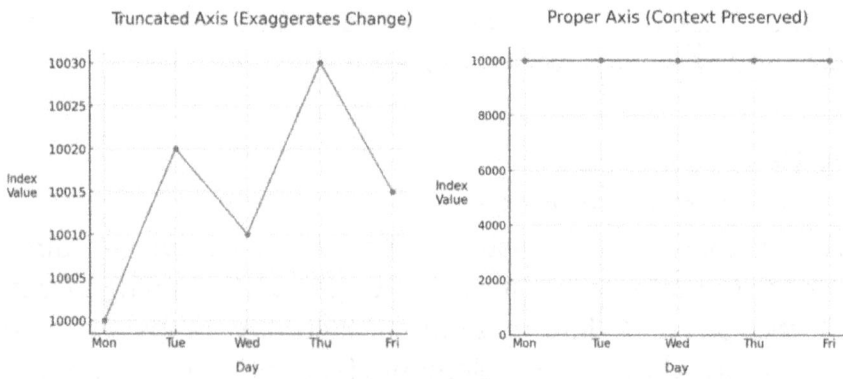

Truncated axis (left): By starting the y-axis at 10,000 instead of 0, the same small changes suddenly look like dramatic spikes and crashes.

Normal axis (right): With the y-axis starting at 0, the stock market fluctuations look minor.

In the next chapter, we'll shift gears and explore the practical techniques and platforms that help you bring your stories to life, from data prep to visualization.

Key takeaways

• Simplicity builds clarity and trust—high signal, low noise.

• Color guides attention but must be used sparingly, consistently, and with cultural and tonal awareness.

• Accessibility and scale are critical—design for all viewers and avoid misleading axes or distorted visuals.

• Visual thinking is empathy: you are designing for your audience, not for yourself.

8

TOOLS & TECHNIQUES

By now, you've learned how to shape a story from data, including how to interpret the data, find insight, build a narrative, and choose the right visuals. The next step in data storytelling takes place through software, platforms, and workflows that convert your ideas from raw data to polished communication.

This chapter is about the "how" and the practical side of storytelling with data and how the right tools can make your ideas easier to express. We won't go too deep into specific software—both because the landscape evolves rapidly and because the principles matter more than the particular tool you decide to use. What's most important is knowing how to choose and apply the right techniques to bring clarity and impact to your story.

Start with the data: organizing for clarity

Before you can tell a great story, your data needs to be structured in a way that supports analysis and insight. This means clean, consistent, and organized data.

Spreadsheets, like Excel or Google Sheets, are still the go-to starting point for most people and for good reason: they're flexible, visual, and familiar. But their power only shows when used with intention. This means:

- Each column should represent a single variable
- Each row should represent a single observation

- No merged cells, no manual formatting embedded in the data
- Clear, consistent naming conventions

A messy dataset is like a cluttered desk; it makes it harder to think clearly. Whether you're working in Sheets, SQL, or Python, cleanliness is the first step toward clarity. For more complex or structured data, tools like Airtable, Notion databases, or data warehouses (like BigQuery or Snowflake) can help manage and organize information.

Get to know your data

Before you can tell a story, you have to understand the material you're working with. This is where exploratory data analysis (EDA) comes in.

Exploratory data analysis is the stage where you "get to know" your dataset. Rather than jumping straight to conclusions, you poke, prod, and play with the numbers. This means looking for anomalies, clusters, gaps, or surprising relationships.

At this stage, it's important to distinguish exploratory from explanatory analysis.

- **Exploratory analysis** is about generating questions. Think of it as wandering through the data with a flashlight. You're exploring the unknown, testing hypotheses, and mapping the terrain.
- **Explanatory analysis** is about answering questions. Once you've discovered what's meaningful, you refine, validate, and package those insights into clear explanations for others. Here, you're guiding your audience with a map rather than showing them the whole forest.

Tools like Anvaka's graph visualizer (https://anvaka.github.io/) are useful tools for exploratory data analysis. By plotting relationships in sprawling, interactive networks, you can see connections that would be nearly impossible to detect in raw spreadsheets.

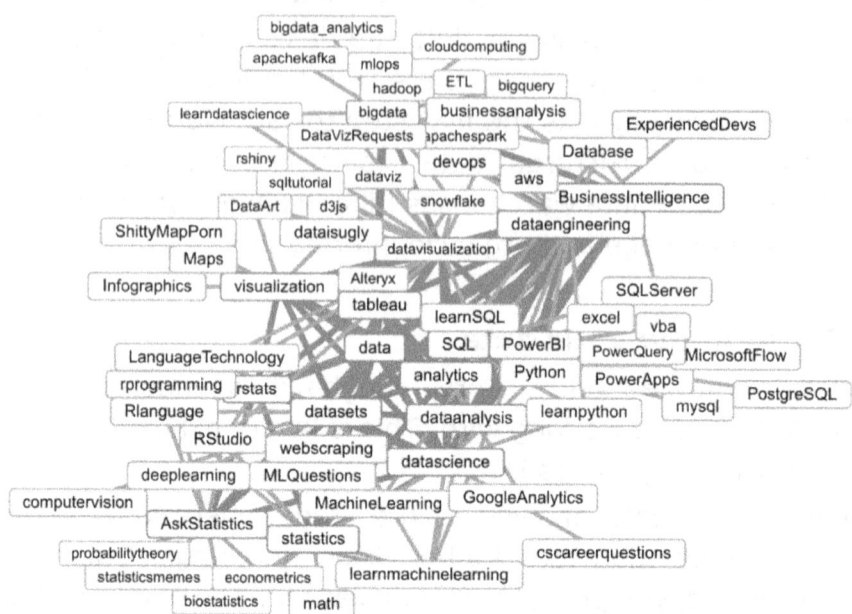

As shown in the example above, Anvaka's tool maps out relationships between subreddits based on where users tend to post or comment across communities. If the same people are active in two different subreddits, those subreddits are drawn closer together and connected by a line. The more overlap, the stronger or thicker the connection. This helps uncover the overall landscape and relationships, which you can then distill into insights and stories for your audience.

Visualizing insights

When it comes to actually telling the story, the tools you use to visualize and communicate matter because they shape how others receive the message.

For most professionals, tools like PowerPoint, Google Slides, Canva, or Keynote are the primary storytelling software. Use them to build a clear narrative, one slide per idea, with clean charts and deliberate flow. If you need more advanced or interactive visuals, tools like Flourish, Datawrapper, Charticulator, or Observable allow for custom designs and web-friendly storytelling. These platforms are ideal when you want to embed stories online or share with a broader, less technical audience.

Whatever you use, keep your focus on the message over the mechanics. A simple bar chart that tells a clear story is more powerful than a fancy interactive dashboard no one understands.

Flourish for template-driven storytelling

One of the most powerful no-code storytelling software platforms is Flourish, which hosts a library of interactive templates that transform static data into engaging, web-friendly stories. The best thing about Flourish is its accessibility: you don't need code or advanced design skills to produce professional, interactive stories that are ready to embed online or share with stakeholders.

While it offers dozens of template types, it is best known for popularizing the bar chart race—an animated chart that shows categories rising and falling in rank over time.

To create a bar chart race in Flourish, your dataset needs at least three elements: a time dimension (e.g., year, month), categories (e.g., countries, products, companies), and a numeric value (e.g., revenue, population, followers). With this tidy structure—one row per category per time period—Flourish animates the shifting rankings automatically.

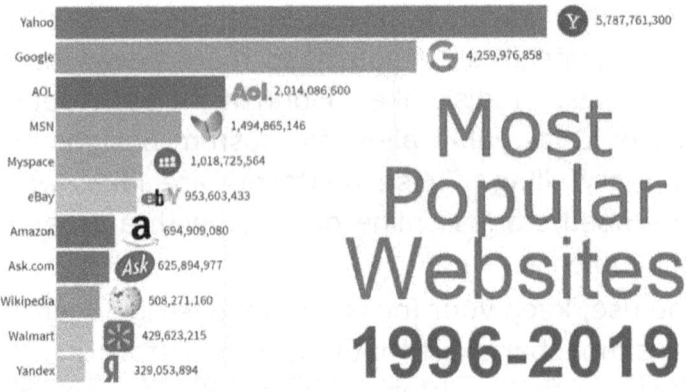

Flourish also supports the creation of line chart races. Instead of bars shifting position over time, line chart races show lines moving from left to right across the chart as their positions change, making them especially effective for tracking trends or rankings.

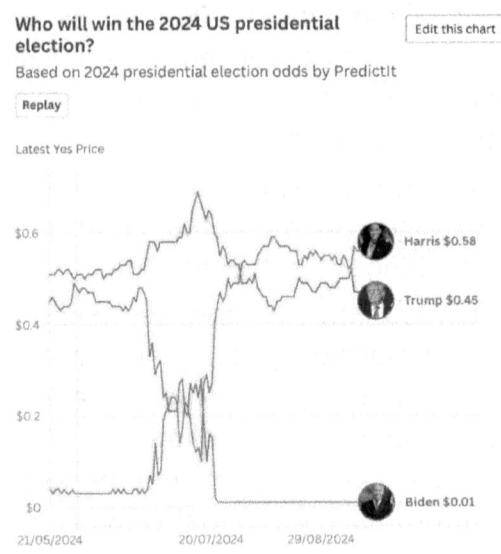

This line chart race, for instance, visualizes the rise and fall of polling data for candidates in a presidential election, clearly revealing shifts in betting odds as the campaign unfolds over several months.

Beyond races, Flourish offers a wide range of templates, including projection maps (geographic data with regions or coordinates), line projections (time series with future scenarios), and survey charts (categorical breakdowns). Each template comes with a source dataset you can view, giving you a blueprint for how to prepare your own data. A bar chart race template, for instance, will expect time-series values with categories that change rank over periods. A line projection chart requires at least one variable plotted against time, plus optional comparison series or confidence intervals. By examining the structure of these source data files, you can then reverse-engineer what data is required.

Below is an example with the projection map on the left and a snippet of source data on the right.

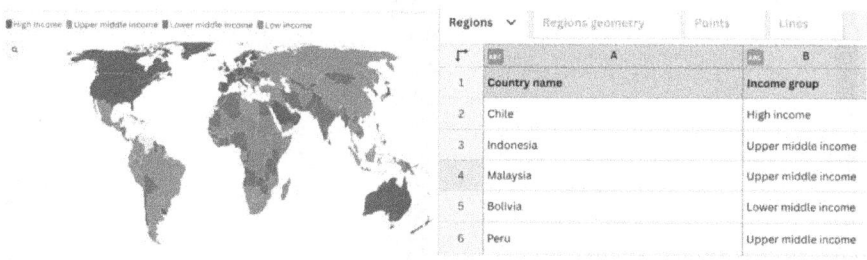

Projection maps like this let you visualize geographic patterns. This could be election results, sales by region, or climate data across countries. To create a projection map, your dataset will need a geographic identifier (such as country names, ISO country codes, or latitude/longitude coordinates) paired with a value to map (like percentage of votes, revenue, or temperature). The template then shades or colors regions to show intensity, making spatial patterns immediately obvious for the audience to understand.

To get started with Flourish, you can browse their free online training videos to guide you through building different types of charts at:

https://training.flourish.studio/courses/flourish-beginner

Instachart for quick visualization

Instachart, a free tool created by Luzmo, is built for creating quick, shareable data visualizations without the steep learning curve of professional software. It allows users to upload a dashboard screenshot, a Figma mockup, or even a simple hand-drawn sketch, and instantly converts it into a working dashboard. This AI-powered approach dramatically accelerates the design process, helping you move quickly from concept to prototype.

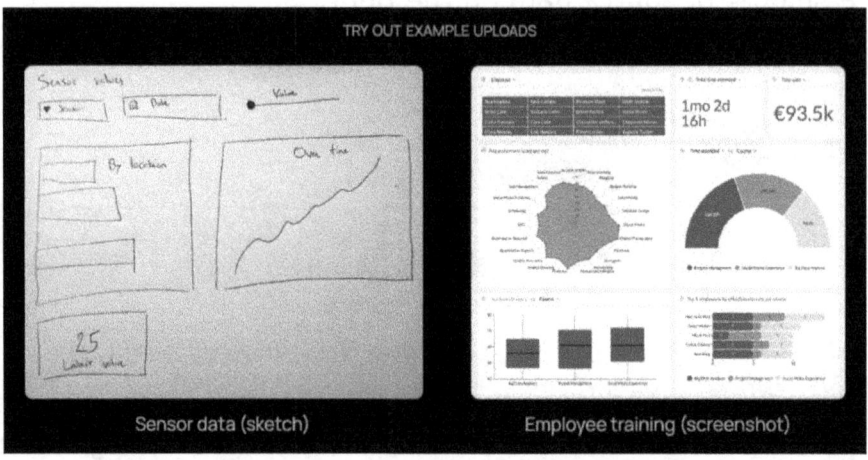

Instachart supports a range of visualization types, from bar and line charts to more narrative-friendly forms such as timelines and annotated trend lines. One of Instachart's key features is its ability to auto-generate dummy data for the dashboard. This gives creators a realistic preview of how the final product will look, even before connecting live metrics. When the design is ready, the placeholder data can be replaced with actual business numbers. By removing the need for coding or complex setup in the early stages, this lowers the barrier to entry for dashboard creation and helps product builders iterate faster.

Instachart also works well for data storytelling. Each chart can be annotated directly, allowing you to highlight turning points, call out comparisons, or explain what a trend means. As the charts are hosted online, they can be shared with a link or embedded, which helps maintain consistency across teams and platforms. That said, Instachart isn't meant for deep exploration or advanced analysis.

ChatGPT for rough visualization

ChatGPT is great for rapid chart prototypes. ChatGPT uses Matplotlib, which is a Python library for data visualization, useful for generating most static charts (line, bar, scatter, heatmaps, etc.). Using ChatGPT, you can paste a data table or upload a CSV file, request a chart type (bar, line, scatter, heatmap), and get a usable first draft within seconds. That speed is perfect for exploring narrative angles or mocking up charts.

Two things you must always verify yourself when using ChatGPT are scale and numbers. Check that axes and tick marks match your intent (e.g., bars start at zero; time runs left to right with consistent intervals; units and rounding are correct). You will also need to cross-check every plotted value against your source data.

If you notice ChatGPT repeating the same mistakes, like cramped layouts or insufficient whitespace, you can fix this in your prompt. You can do this by being explicit about margins, spacing, label orientation, and annotation style. You can also ask ChatGPT to "generate charts following best data storytelling and visualization practices" to reduce errors by default (clear labels, direct line labeling, accessible colors, minimal clutter, and honest scales).

Sample prompt
Using the data below, create a [chart type]. Start the y-axis at zero (if appropriate), put time on the x-axis with equal intervals, label axes with units, add concise titles, avoid 3D or heavy textures, use one bold highlight with muted context, ensure ample whitespace (no rotated text), and include annotations for the key peak and trough. Then list the exact values plotted so I can verify.

One last reminder: tools are just tools
It's easy to get caught up in which platform is best or what new tool everyone is using. But remember: your audience doesn't care how you made the chart—they care what it means. This means you don't need a fancy tool to tell a powerful story. You need to focus on clarity, intention, and empathy because the best data stories are the ones that help someone make a better decision, regardless of the software used to create them.

Key takeaways
- Clean, organized data is the foundation of any good story and clarity starts at the dataset level.
- Exploratory analysis helps you get to know your data, revealing patterns, gaps, and surprises.
- Platforms like Flourish offer templates that can turn raw numbers into dynamic, engaging narratives.
- The visualization tool is secondary; clarity, intention, and empathy are what ultimately make data stories impactful.

9

PRESENTING

There comes a moment when your data story has to leave your head and dashboard and present itself in the real world. Most often, that happens in a slide deck or a written report. These formats are the vehicles that carry your insights to decision-makers, stakeholders, clients, or teammates. Just like any good vehicle, they need to be well-designed, purposeful, and easy to steer.

Unfortunately, this is where many data stories fall apart. Most data stories fail from overload. Instead of one clear insight, they bury the audience under every possible data point. Remember: what you cut is as important as what you show. If you approach your slides and reports as storytelling tools, not just documentation tools, you can dramatically strengthen your impact.

The first principle is one idea per slide. Each slide should carry a single message and not five takeaways. Not three different charts. One clear point. Anything more creates visual noise and splits attention. If you have multiple points to make, break them into multiple slides. Let each one breathe. This might feel inefficient at first. But in reality, it makes communication faster because the audience doesn't have to work hard to figure out what you're trying to say.

Along with a single message, your slides should follow a logical flow—a beginning, middle, and end. Start with context, build tension, and resolve with insight. Revisit the core takeaway at the close. You're guiding the audience through a narrative journey.

Headlines matter more than people think. Don't settle for vague titles like "Sales Performance" or "User Feedback." Make your headlines carry insight: "Sales Declined in Q2 Despite Increased Ad Spend" or "User Complaints Centered Around Mobile Checkout Experience." A headline should tell the story even if the rest of the slide is skipped.

When it comes to charts, simpler is better. Use clear axes. Use color sparingly. Use labels that explain what's happening. If the audience needs to pause to figure out what they're looking at, you've already lost momentum.

Then there's text. Slides are not scripts, so be concise and keep bullet points to a minimum. If you must include commentary or background detail, place it in speaker notes or supporting materials. Also, be mindful of how text is displayed. Avoid awkward placements like 45° or 90° angles, which force people to tilt their heads or strain their eyes. Text should be clear and legible, even from the back of a large room. A good test is this: can someone glance at your slide for three seconds and understand the main message? If not, the text needs to be reduced or repositioned.

If you're writing a report instead of a slide deck, the principles still apply, but the format shifts. In a written report, paragraphs replace visuals more often, and there's room for more detailed context or explanation. Still, every section should have a clear purpose. Visual hierarchy matters in documents, too. Use headers, subheaders, bold text, whitespace, and formatting to guide the reader's attention. A wall of text is just as overwhelming as a cluttered slide.

Whether you're presenting live or sending materials asynchronously, remember that the audience experience is everything. In a live setting, you have the benefit of voice and body language. You can pace your delivery, add emphasis, and adjust on the fly. In a static report, your words and visuals do all the work—so they have to be precise and intentional.

When presenting live, practice matters. Remember that pacing, pausing, and even silence are as powerful as visuals—they give your audience space to absorb the message and emphasize what matters most. But keep in mind: your visuals are there to support you, not compete with you. Don't read from the screen. Use the slides to reinforce your spoken message.

In a written document, your writing style becomes your voice. Be human, clear, and avoid jargon unless it's expected by your audience. Use plain language to make your insights accessible, no matter how complex the data is behind them.

Lastly, always end strong. Whether it's a slide or a report, your final page should be more than a thankyou. Use it to reinforce the key takeaway, highlight the next step, and leave your audience with clarity, not questions.

Scrollytelling

Instead of a slide presentation, where you control the pace by clicking through and explaining each point as part of a live presentation, there are times when it's more effective to let the audience guide themselves through the story.

Scrollytelling—short for scroll plus storytelling—is one way of presenting digital stories to a non-live audience while still creating a deep sense of immersion and discovery. Instead of speaking directly to an audience, information is displayed digitally and delivered gradually at the reader's own pace. Visuals and text appear, move, disappear, or change as the user scrolls down the page. A chart might animate to reveal changes over time, a map might update to highlight different regions, or a visualization might shift perspective to show a new dimension of the same data.

The key strength of scrollytelling is that it combines narrative with interactivity. Instead of overwhelming the audience with a wall of numbers or a dense dashboard, each movement of the page acts like a cue, pulling the reader deeper into the story while introducing new context at just the right moment. This makes complex data feel more approachable, as the story comes alive in stages, building anticipation and clarity.

To ensure the story unfolds gradually, each chart or map should emphasize only the insight relevant to that moment. A bar chart might begin in grayscale, for example, and then animate into color to spotlight the most important category. A map might zoom from a global view into a specific region as the text introduces the detail.

Lastly, it's essential to give the reader a smooth user experience. Unlike presentation slides, you're not clicking forward for them, so the story needs to have smooth transitions and responsive behavior across devices, as jerky or lagging visuals can break the immersive effect. This involves testing how the story feels on desktop and mobile, including different operating systems and browsers.

To get started with scrollytelling, software like Flourish (https://flourish.studio/visualisations/scrollytelling/) comes with ready-made templates that let you pair text with dynamic charts or maps. You can then publish and embed stories on a web page without needing any coding skills.

Common mistakes & how to fix them

Even the best data storytellers slip up. Under pressure to deliver, it's easy to fall into habits that derail your message: cluttered visuals, overexplaining, stretching the truth, or forgetting your audience. These mistakes can weaken your story, erode trust, and prevent action.

The good news is that most mistakes are easily fixable. The first step is recognizing them. The second is having the discipline to revise. The next section is your guide to common pitfalls in data storytelling and how to avoid them.

Mistake 1: Over-relying on AI

While AI tools excel at recognizing patterns in complex data and quickly generating visual charts, they still lack the human judgment to know what should be prioritized and how best to package the content for a specific audience. AI tools are also susceptible to making basic mistakes with numbers and chart design.

Solution: Treat AI as an assistant, not an author. Use it to speed up analysis, generate options, or visualize possibilities, but reserve the final decisions for yourself. Bring in context, empathy, and domain expertise to shape the narrative. The best results come from a partnership: AI for scale and speed, humans for insight and storytelling.

Mistake 2: Showing everything you found

You've spent hours combing through the data testing segments, cleaning messy columns, and chasing anomalies. Naturally, you want to show the full journey. But your audience didn't take that journey with you. If you show everything, you risk overwhelming them or burying the point you want to make.

Solution: Edit ruthlessly. Ask yourself, "What's the one thing I want them to remember?" Keep that and cut the rest or move it to an appendix.

Mistake 3: Inconsistent visuals

You want to be creative and showcase your full visualization repertoire by using multiple chart types and color schemes or redesigning the layout on every slide. The result may look impressive, but to the audience, it feels inconsistent and confusing. Instead of focusing on the insight, they're forced to constantly re-learn how to read each chart. Inconsistency creates friction and distracts from the insight.

Solution: Avoid switching between multiple chart types to show the same data unless necessary. Likewise, keep colors, labels, and design choices consistent so your audience doesn't have to re-learn how to read each new visual.

Mistake 4: Hiding the insight

You've done the analysis, made the chart, and designed the slides, but you never quite say what it all means. The data is there, but the conclusion isn't. You expect people to connect the dots themselves but they won't—not because they're not smart, but because it's not their job to do so.

Solution: State the insight clearly. Use the slide title, a bold takeaway, or a callout box. Make it impossible to miss the point. If you had to sum up the message in a sentence, what would it be? Put that sentence front and center.

Mistake 5: Letting bias drive the story

It's tempting to build stories that confirm what stakeholders want to hear. This might involve overstating the results or ignoring data that doesn't support the intended narrative. A story that lacks integrity can still be persuasive, but it won't be trusted for long.

Solution: Be transparent about your findings, show uncertainty when it exists, and include caveats or assumptions where necessary. By doing so, you're not actually weakening your story, but strengthening trust and credibility with your audience.

Mistake 6: Misunderstanding your audience

You know your data inside out, but your audience might not. They may not be analysts. They may not care about p-values or standard deviations. If you assume too much background knowledge, your message won't land. On the flip side, oversimplifying for an expert audience can come across as patronizing or vague. The key, therefore, is balance.

Solution: Tailor your story and speak their language. Adjust your visuals, detail level, and tone based on who you're talking to. If you're unsure, test it. Share a draft with a colleague who knows the audience better than you do and have them articulate to you where their eyes focus, what they see, what observations they draw, and what questions they ask.

Mistake 7: Ending without action

You've walked them through the analysis. You've shown the insight. But when it's time to wrap up, your story just ends. No next step, no recommendation, and no clarity about what's supposed to happen next.

Solution: Always land the story. What should the audience do with what they've learned? Should they approve a budget? Investigate further? Change course? Summarize the takeaway, and make the action obvious.

Key takeaways

- One idea per slide—clarity beats clutter.
- Structure matters: context, tension, insight, resolution.
- Headlines should tell the story.
- In live settings, slides support your voice; in reports, your writing is the voice.
- Scrollytelling transforms data into an immersive journey, revealing insights step by step at the reader's own pace.

- Always end with impact—state the action or next step, not just "thank you."

10

FROM ANALYST TO INFLUENCER

We started this book with a simple idea: data alone isn't enough. The world doesn't need more dashboards. It needs more meaning, more clarity, and more stories that cut through the noise and help more people make better decisions.

You've learned that storytelling with data is not just about charts, it's about choices. The choice to ask better questions. To prioritize insight over information, to speak your audience's language, to reduce clutter, and to build narratives that guide, not just report.

You've also learnt that storytelling is a strategic skill that accelerates understanding and changes outcomes. If you've followed the path this book has laid out, you already know the key ingredients: direction, structure, clarity, audience awareness, narrative discipline, data literacy, good visuals, and strong presentation skills. But to turn that into influence, you need one more thing: trust.

Trust is built when people consistently walk away from your presentations or reports thinking, "That was useful. That made sense. I know what to do next." When your audience feels guided rather than overwhelmed, you establish yourself as someone who adds clarity, not confusion.

You also don't build trust by showing off how smart you are. Overloading a slide with jargon, complex models, or endless numbers may demonstrate technical skill, but it leaves people feeling lost or excluded. Real trust comes when you flip the perspective: your goal isn't to make yourself look impressive, but to make your audience feel empowered. This means translating complexity into something manageable. You highlight the signal, not the noise. You connect the dots in a way others hadn't considered. You give people confidence that they can take the next step with clarity. Each time you help your audience see what they couldn't see before, you earn credibility.

Over time, that credibility compounds. People begin to view you not just as an analyst or presenter, but as a trusted advisor—someone whose insights can influence strategy, shape decisions, and set direction. That's what earns you a seat at the table, not just as a participant, but as a voice people want to hear.

And, hopefully, you've come to realize that this skill isn't reserved for "creative types" or "design people." It's for analysts, strategists, marketers, product managers, scientists, executives—*anyone* who works with data and wants to make an impact.

After all, you don't have to master every tool or memorize every chart type. But if you remember the fundamentals of starting with the right question, serving your audience, simplifying the message, and guiding with structure, you will be ahead of 90% of professionals working with data today.

Remember to stay curious, too. Study great communicators, even outside the world of data. Learn what makes people care, what keeps their attention, and what moves them to act. Every presentation is a chance to test and improve. And perhaps most importantly: teach what you learn. Share your process with your team. Offer to review others' slides. Help colleagues tell better stories. When you raise the level of data communication around you, you amplify your own impact.

Because here's the truth: storytelling with data isn't a solo skill—it's a culture. When people see data not as a wall of numbers, but as a story they can engage with, the whole organization starts making better decisions. It becomes faster, smarter, and more aligned.

So keep practicing, keep refining, and keep telling stories worth listening to. Your data has something to say, and the world is waiting to hear it, clearly.

TEMPLATES

Insight Slide
Slide title: Insight as a sentence (e.g., *"Mobile users dropped off after the pricing update"*)
Visual: One chart or key number
Footer: Recommended action or implication

Comparison Slide
Title: State what the comparison shows
Left: Visual A (e.g., before or Group A)
Right: Visual B (e.g., after or Group B)
Bottom: Summary sentence + next step

Narrative Flow (Multi-slide)
Slide 1: Context ("Here's where we started")
Slide 2: Tension ("Here's the problem/change")
Slide 3: Insight ("Here's what we found")
Slide 4: Resolution ("Here's what we recommend")

CHECKLIST

Use this before finalizing any data presentation, report, or visualization.

Story & audience
- Have I clearly defined the key question?
- Do I know what my audience needs to hear—not just what I want to say?
- Have I built a narrative with a beginning, middle, and end?
- Does my story have a captivating hook?
- Is there a single takeaway per slide or section?

Charts & visuals
- Have I selected the best chart type for the message?
- Are axes, labels, and units clearly marked?
- Have I removed unnecessary gridlines, colors, and effects?
- Is my key insight visually emphasized?

Design & layout
- Is there a visual hierarchy? (What do I want them to see first?)
- Have I used whitespace and alignment for clarity?
- Are fonts and colors consistent throughout?

Language & tone
- Are headlines insight-driven (not just labels)?
- Have I removed jargon and simplified language for my audience?
- Does the tone match the stakes of the story?

Call-to-action
- Have I clearly stated what the audience should do next?
- If applicable, have I included supporting details in the appendix or backup slides?

PRACTICE EXERCISES

1. The One-Message Slide
- Take a cluttered dashboard or report page.
- Redesign it as a single-slide story with one insight, one chart, and one action.
- Present it in 30 seconds as a short video.

2. Chart Makeover Challenge
- Provide participants with a poorly designed chart (e.g., a messy pie chart or confusing bar chart).
- Ask them to recreate it using a better chart type and visual clarity principles.
- Compare versions and discuss design decisions.

3. Audience Flip
- Choose one data story.
- Create two different versions: one for a C-level exec, one for a technical analyst.
- Discuss what changed and why.

4. Narrative Mapping
- Give participants a dataset and a loose business question (e.g., "Why are customer renewals down?")
- Have them map out a 4-slide story arc: context, tension, insight, recommendation.

5. Live Story Debugging
- Show an example of a confusing or misleading data slide.
- As a group, identify what's wrong, rewrite the headline, choose a new chart, and rewrite the narrative.

OTHER BOOKS BY THE AUTHOR

Generative AI Art for Beginners
Master the use of text prompts to generate stunning AI art in seconds.

ChatGPT Prompt Engineering Book
Learn the art of precision prompt writing, including negative prompting, role prompts, and prompt boundaries to 3X your productivity using ChatGPT.

AI for Absolute Beginners
This book is the complete guide for beginners to AI, including easy-to-follow breakdowns of natural language processing, generative AI, deep learning, recommender systems, and computer vision.

Machine Learning for Absolute Beginners
Learn the fundamentals of machine learning, as explained in plain English.

Machine Learning with Python for Beginners
Progress your career in machine learning by learning how to code in Python and build your own prediction models to solve real-life problems.

Machine Learning: Make Your Own Recommender System
Learn how to make your own machine learning recommender system in an afternoon using Python.

Data Analytics for Absolute Beginners
Make better decisions using every variable with this deconstructed introduction to data analytics.

Statistics for Absolute Beginners
Master the fundamentals of inferential and descriptive statistics with a mix of practical demonstrations, visual examples, historical origins, and plain English explanations.

www.ingramcontent.com/pod-product-compliance
Ingram Content Group UK Ltd.
Pitfield, Milton Keynes, MK11 3LW, UK
UKHW021317081025
8297UKWH00014B/59